CW00430315

Introducing Knitting

Introducing Knitting

Audrie Stratford

B T Batsford Limited London
Drake Publishers Inc New York

© Audrie Stratford 1972
First published 1972
ISBN 0 7134 2430 3
Library of Congress Catalog Card Number 79-175963
Reprinted 1972

Filmset by Filmtype Services Limited, Scarborough, Yorkshire
Printed in Great Britain by Anchor Press
and bound by William Brendon Limited
for the publishers
B T Batsford Limited
4 Fitzhardinge Street, London W1 and
Drake Publishers Inc
381 Park Avenue South, New York, NY 10016

Contents

Acknowledgment

It gives me great pleasure to offer my thanks to Miss H A Fulford, Mr D Prosser, Miss J Randall and Mrs C Whittley, all of whom, in their various capacities, have kindly commented on the script and offered much stimulating advice.

Mr R Willis has been assiduous in the difficult task of illustrating the contortions of a knitted strand and Thelma M Nye of Batsfords has been patient and understanding every stitch of the way.

The Bennals
Kings Lynn 1972   A S

Good knitting made easy

Paradoxically, the difficulty about knitting is its simplicity.

It is so easy that beginners are tempted to rush ahead un-critically, picking up bad habits and reinforcing them by repetition. Surprisingly, some teachers think they need do no more than show a child how to make knit and purl stitches and to cast on and off. Knitting is easy, but good knitting is not as easy as all that, and this book sets out to show how, if care is taken, it can be both easy and good.

Some people start by thinking that the individual details of knitting are too small to worry about, but the very first garment they make should teach them the most important lesson of all— that there is no short cut to excellence. The only way to knit well is to take trouble with every stitch.

No-one can learn knitting just by reading about it. All begin-ners must take up their needles and knit; those who intend to knit well must make a critical study of all that they do with their needles. They must investigate . . . study each manipula-tion separately, experiment with trial pieces, test effects, observe results and finally, examine relationships between processes by incorporating each in turn into a whole garment. This disciplined study, based on fundamentals, can help many experienced knitters as well, for unpredictable gaps are almost inevitable in knowledge picked up piecemeal.

How to use this book

This book deliberately treats knitting as if it were a totally unfamiliar craft. The pages should, in the first instance, be studied in strict sequence for a few new words and methods have been introduced where current habit seems inadequate or unpopular. All terms have been defined where they first occur in the text (as well as in the Glossary which starts on page 150). The aims of all procedures have been stated at the beginning of each description so that knitters can judge, in samplers, the success of the manipulation.

The ideal 'sampler' for young learners is a set of dolls' clothes but adults need to do plenty of stitchmaking if their movements are to be perfected, so a full-sized garment is better for them. No single standard garment involves all normal knitting processes but the sleeveless pullover, which is the basis of this book, has been specially designed to include as many manipulations as possible, in a convenient order. It is shown on page 143 and its pattern, set out in two different ways, on pages 144 to 147, both kinds of layout being explained in the text. All the processes needed for its making are described in detail in the order of their occurrence in the instructions so text and pattern are parallel and should be used alternately. In the text the sign † indicates that a set of descriptions has been completed and the newly acquired skills should next be worked into the garment. Once knitting has started, an unfamiliar instruction should take the knitter from the garment back to the text until the next set of skills has been mastered.

Some of the descriptions do not refer directly to the pullover but even these should be carefully studied in sequence for they help explain processes which are used in it. In any case, they are used in standard knitting and will be needed in making socks and gloves. The patterns for these, on pages 148 and 149, are given in outline only and each knitter must fill in her own numbers, obtained from calculations based on the size and shape of the particular garment required. This gives the perfection of fit which should characterise hand-made garments. When the knitter has learnt to make these calculations successfully she should be able to modify bought leaflets sufficiently to guarantee perfect fit, to bring individuality to an otherwise standard garment or simply to make the instructions easier to work.

The book gives the information necessary for straightforward illustrated leaflets to be followed but its real aim is to stimulate knitters to investigate everything for themselves, this being the most effective way of improving the craft and their enjoyment of it. Knitters have the unusual advantage of both making and fashioning their basic fabric so they have absolute control over shape, style, size and thickness. They also have a wide choice of colours, materials and fabrics which they can combine into rich textures and designs, giving experienced knitters almost unlimited scope for invention. Learners, too, can produce good results if from the beginning they aim at perfection. Care taken at the start is rewarded in the end by great personal enjoyment and satisfaction.

Metrication

Knitting is a useful aid to numeracy for though knitters use formal units of measurement only when they are estimating the amount or thickness of yarn or the size of stitches, they count rows and columns at every stage of their work and often have to set these stitches out in groups such as the four parts of most garments or the repeats which make up decorative fabrics. These repeats usually involve 2, 3, 4, 6, 8 or 9 stitches and only rarely five or ten so knitters are apt to think in duo-decimals. However, as everyone should understand decimal usage both methods are described, in this book, whenever exact units are being considered.

Hints on learning knitting

1 Study it as though it were totally unfamiliar.

2 Try to apply the principles of time and motion study. There are several thousand stitches in most garments so even the slightest waste of energy or time in making a single stitch soon adds up to an impressive total.

3 Study every detail connected with it. Study the yarn, the tools and the knitted fabrics. Feel them. Draw the stitches. When knitting, listen to the click of the needles and notice the pull of the yarn against stitches, needles and hands. Try to explain every change.

4 Expend time liberally in the early stages; it pays in the end.

5 Make frequent tests of stitchmaking and keep the test pieces as a record of progress toward excellence.

6 Investigate using the minimum number of stitches (to save time), thick needles (so that all aspects of each stitch can be thoroughly examined) and scraps of yarn (kept handy for the purpose). Later, try different thicknesses of needles and of yarn and notice how the differences affect the results. Finally, practise the manipulation using plenty of stitches and the most helpful yarn and needles.

7 Never tolerate mistakes in the final knitting. Undo the work and re-knit it without the mistake. Knitting yarn need not betray re-use.

8 As each procedure is mastered, record it in a sampler.

9 Keep a Record Book and make full use of it. Keep in it the samplers, annotated for reference; also the test pieces recording progress in stitchmaking; examples of different fabrics; details about garments which have been knitted; and anything else which might be helpful.

10 Start real knitting with something relatively small, but usable.

Knitting yarns

Anything knittable can be regarded as knitting yarn and there is no such thing as a bad yarn: nor are there good yarns, as such. Yarns are simply right or wrong for a particular job and it is up to the knitter to choose the one which is most suitable.

Real understanding of yarn comes only with use, but much can be learnt from a collection staged perhaps by members of a school or of a club. This might include:

a all kinds of knittable strands such as man-made yarns and those from plants, narrow ribbon and strips of metal foil, string and raffia, solid strands of plastic and spirally-cut nylon stockings as well as orthodox knitting wools;

b something made from each yarn to show off its special characteristics;

c the band or label, if any, from the yarn;

d older and current pattern leaflets.

All bands and labels carry printed information and most also have a mark, called the vat number or dye lot, which distinguishes that batch of yarn from all others, whether it has been dyed or bleached or is any kind of mixture. All balls used in a garment should carry the same mark on the labels, for if yarn which seems similar but which comes from a different batch is used in the same area of knitting, the difference shows up vividly. Many retailers will set aside for a customer more yarn from the same batch than is likely to be wanted for a garment and she can buy from this as she needs. This 'lay-by' service is free, but as it is uneconomical for yarn to be long out of working stock, retailers ask to be told when no more of it is needed.

The leaflets may be reminders that named yarns belong to the fashion world and do not always stay long on the market. Learners should play safe when choosing a pattern leaflet, making sure the named yarn is readily available. Experienced knitters will do well to experiment, not only using modern yarns in place of apparently similar ones which are no longer available, but also trying unfamiliar ones. It may be risky but the risk is worth taking, for a successful result can be impressive.

Whenever instructions are followed using a substitute yarn similar to the original, the garment should fit equally well and take a similar *length* of yarn but as its *weight* may be very different the number of balls required may need careful calculation or the use of the lay-by service.

Constituent materials of knitting yarns

The animal, plant and mineral materials which make up knitting yarns feel different from one another and behave differently. Mixtures are different again and there are potentially so many of them that experience is the only adequate guide to their characteristics. Nevertheless, each group of materials has many properties in common.

Synthetics Rayon, nylon and terylene were among the first to be invented, but others may yet become popular and all may be produced in various forms.

They are apt to attract dirt due to static electricity but are easy to wash and dry. Shrinkage is rarely a problem but sometimes garments stretch when dry cleaned and even when carefully washed.

Plant products eg cotton and linen, do not attract dirt, are easy to wash, but are slow to dry and sometimes shrink a little.

Animal yarns apart from silk, are almost all made from the hair of various mammals, the most important being wool. Merino sheep produce a luxurious wool, soft, non-irritating and pleasant to handle. It knits up evenly but needs careful washing for it tends to become felted and to shrink. It is often called *Botany wool* in recognition of the importance of Botany Bay (near Sydney) when Australia, still the main producer, first exported this wool.

Most other wool is termed *crossbred* though the sheep which produce it now mostly belong to pure-bred strains. It is strong and wears well. It is unlikely to shrink or felt and it is springy in texture rather than obedient. It is used for most traditional knitting such as Aran and Sanquhar.

Knitting yarns can also be produced from other animal materials. *Angora wool,* from the angora rabbit, is soft, unusually fluffy and looks very attractive. Its disadvantage is that the fibres responsible for the fluffiness are very easily shed, marking the knitter's clothing and her surroundings, and able to irritate and even choke an infant if used in baby-wear.

Alpaca, made from the hairs of a South African llama, is thin and so stiff that when knitted normally it always looks untidy but if suitably worked the stitches can be made to spring out into circles.

Mohair, made from the hair of certain goats, is often brushed to make a yarn with such an irregular surface that the structure of the fabric is almost obscured.

Investigating the structure of knitting yarns

The behaviour of a knitting yarn is affected not only by its constituents but also by its structure. Choose any yarn and study the tactile characteristics such as softness, smoothness, springiness etc. which together are termed its *handle*.

Study the visible structure of short pieces of the yarn.

1 Notice the twist, or spin. *Is it regular, tight, loose?* Twist a piece tighter. *What happens to the thickness and the handle?* Twist it tighter still. *What happens to the shape?* Let go. *Is it the original thickness?*

2 Pull it lengthways. *Does it disintegrate or stay whole?* Untwist it completely. *What happens to the thickness and the appearance?* Pull it lengthways. *Does it disintegrate or stay whole?*

3 Separate another piece into its plies, ie its component strands. *How closely are they twisted together? Which way?* Pull a ply lengthways. *Does it disintegrate or stay whole?* Untwist it. Pull lengthways. *Does it disintegrate or stay whole?*

4 Use a lens to study the constituent fibres. *Are they parallel or tangled?* Make a rough estimate of their average length; *one centimetre, five, ten?* How many fibres in a cross-section? *Are they counted in tens, hundreds, thousands?* Study their shape. *Are they crimped, loosely waved or straight?*

5 Study the distribution of colour. *Are the plies different, ie marl? Are the fibres within the ply different, ie lovat? Or all the same, ie solid colour? Are successive short lengths of the yarn dyed differently, ie rainbow?*

Find other knitting yarns and examine them in the same ways. Note variations between them in thickness of original yarn; thickness of individual plies; number of plies; tightness of twist; distribution of colour.

Thickness of yarns

Most dressmakers rely more on touch than on measurement when estimating the thickness of cloth, but the thickness of a strand of yarn is so difficult to judge that knitters need to know actual measurements in terms of weight and length. Their unit is based on the maxim 'the thinner it is the further it goes'. For example, an ounce of rug wool may measure only forty yards, but an ounce of the finest lace-wool may measure six hundred yards, so the number of yards in an ounce, ie the yarperoz (abbr *yz*), is an exact and easily measured unit of thickness in which higher numbers indicate finer strands, as they do for sewing cottons. In decimal units the thickness is given by the number of metres in one hundred grammes.

Woollen fibres are short and though synthetic materials are originally made in continuous strands, like silk, they are often crimped and chopped and then, like woollen fibres, converted into long strands by the spinning process. If hard-wearing yarn is wanted, the spin is close and tight, but if warmth is more important than strength, the strand is spun more loosely, to trap air, so it looks thick.

Kept single, any strand soon disintegrates but when two or more are twisted together, the structure of each of the plies is secure. Shetland spinners wind together two thin plies when preparing wools for lace-making, two thick plies to make jumper-weight yarns and two plies of intermediate thickness if the yarn is intended for underwear.

Other spinners have one thin basic ply, which used two-fold makes their thin yarn, and used three or four-fold makes their thicker yarns. Fortunately, the thickness of the basic ply differs sufficiently from spinner to spinner to give the knitter many gradations of thickness within the range of each ply-number, 3-ply wools, for example, varying from 200 yz (almost as thin as some 2-ply wools) to 125 yz (almost as thick as some 4-ply wools).

Many spinners increase their range by making one or two thicker basic plies. *Double Knitting* or DK wools are about 60 yz although there may be only 4, 3 or even just two plies; the thicker types still are sold under various trade names.

Thick yarns soon knit up into large areas when thick tools are used, but these are at first so tiring to hold that adult beginners should be content with DK and younger learners should not be encouraged to use anything thicker than a 4-ply wool.

Knitted fabric and its production

Knitted fabric consists of rows of stitches made by drawing a single length of yarn a loop at a time through successive stitches of a lower row, the rows often being joined into rings to make tubular fabric (for most garments are tubular). There need not be visible joins yet any shape can be made, for stitches can vanish into the fabric or new ones be produced from it, the number in the ring or row affecting width, the number in the columns affecting length.

There are only two basic stitches in knitting but repetition of different arrangements of these two stitches and their derivatives can produce a great variety of fabrics, each with its own characteristic appearance and behaviour; the variety can be further increased by the choice of texture, thickness or colour of yarn; all the fabrics are attractively springy; and finished edges are selvedges so, all in all, knitting is an excellent way of producing garments.

The basic fabric is identical, whether made on complicated factory machinery, a simple frame based on a cotton reel and four strids (or nails), a home knitting machine or the hand-knitter's set of needles. Of all these, machines can undoubtedly knit the fastest, but hand tools are the most versatile. They are simple and light enough to be manipulated even by weak or deformed hands so that many people are recommended to take up knitting in order to strengthen muscles or loosen joints. These people may need to hold their needles in unexpected ways. Unless weakness makes it impossible, the two hands should do the same amount of work, so left-handed people are at no disadvantage and all could hold their tools in the same way, although in fact, there is much individual variation.

That being so, any attempt to start by describing the working details of hand-knitting is apt to become a welter of exceptions, but a description of machine-knitting, shorn of working details, offers a simple introduction to the structure of the fabric and to the way it is produced.

Production of machine-knitted fabric

Latched hooks are the essential part of any knitting machine.

Figure 1a On the *first row,* the yarn is converted into a series of loops, each hanging from the shaft of a needle (or hook).

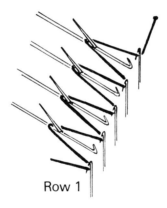

Row 1

Figure 1a

Figure 1b   The *second row* starts with the working end resting across the open hooks. Each hook in turn slides back (away from the knitter) taking the yarn with it through the loop on the shaft so that this slips off the needle onto the front of the work.

Finally the hook slides forward (towards the knitter) until the newly-made loop is hanging on the shaft, all ready to be worked in its turn.

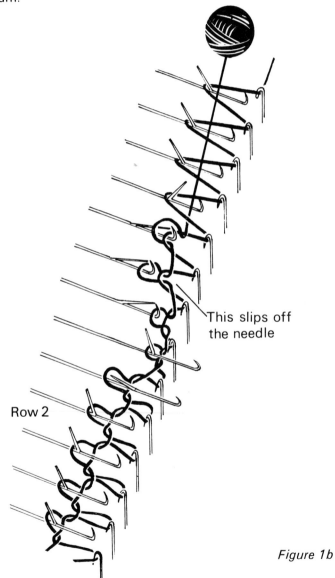

This slips off
the needle

Row 2

Figure 1b

Figure 1c The *third row* is worked in the opposite direction to the second.

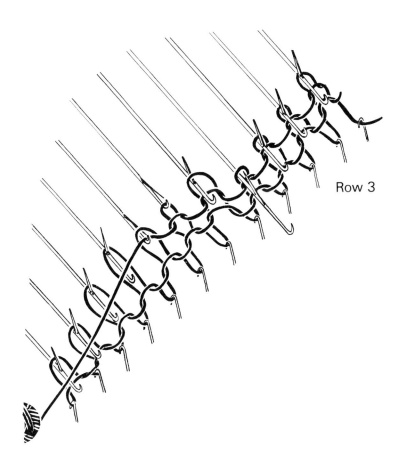

Row 3

Figure 1c

Figure 2a shows that the loops on the top row have not yet been worked; they are open ready to be worked.

Part of three finished rows viewed from front

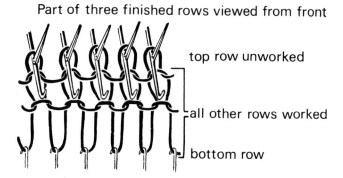

top row unworked

all other rows worked

bottom row

Figure 2a

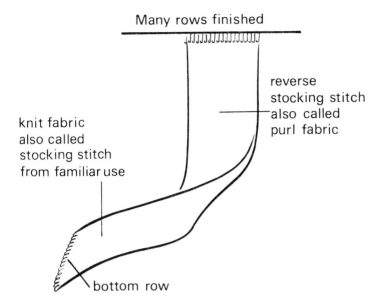

Figure 2b

The effects produced by knitting depend so much upon appearance that if two surfaces look different they may have different names, even if they are known to be obverse and reverse.

Detailed structure of the basic stitch

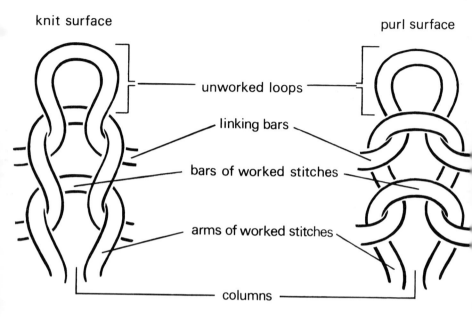

knit surface

purl surface

- unworked loops
- linking bars
- bars of worked stitches
- arms of worked stitches
- columns

Figure 3

Linking bars join every loop and stitch to their immediate neighbours in the row.

Unworked loops (open loops) are normally held on the needle. The two surfaces look the same.

Worked stitches are no longer held on the needle.

The two arms of a worked stitch are the same length, slightly convergent and lie in the same plane. They lie on the knit surface of the worked stitch. The bar of a worked stitch is hinged around the two linking bars of the row above. The bar lies on the purled surface of the worked stitch. The two surfaces look different.

The centres of all bars in a column are *exactly* one above the other.

24

General structure of the surfaces

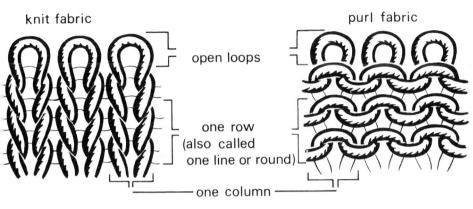

knit fabric   purl fabric

open loops

one row
(also called
one line or round)

one column

Figure 4

Knit fabric is the surface to which the loops are drawn and along which the yarn is *not* carried. In simple machines, the knit surface faces the machine not the knitter, so it is unseen during working.

Purl fabric is the surface from which loops are drawn and along which the yarn *is* carried. It is this surface which faces the operator of the knitting machine.

Knit fabric consists of arms of stitches only, it has a smooth vertical appearance.

Purl fabric consists of bars only, so it has a ridged horizontal look.

Both surfaces look so attractive that either can be used as the 'right' (visible) side of the garment. Clothes made in this and in many other knitted fabrics can be reversible if suitably planned, giving almost two for the price of one.

Machine knitting and hand knitting compared

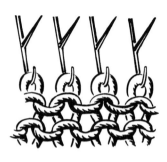
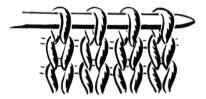

Figure 5

In machine knitting every loop hangs on a separate shaft and all loops are in the same plane as the fabric.

In hand knitting the whole row of loops is held on a continuous shaft, so all loops are twisted across the plane of the fabric.

In machine knitting each loop hangs by its centre so the two arms are the same length and are equally visible during working.

In hand knitting each loop encircles the needle with the left arm hidden behind it so only the right arm, in front of the needle, is easily visible during working.

In machine knitting each loop hangs centrally so the hook automatically draws the new loop under the centre of the bar, therefore, when the worked stitch is set down it necessarily hangs symmetrically around the new loop.

In hand knitting the loop fits so closely around the shaft that the new loop cannot be drawn directly under the bar but has to be made around an arm, usually the front arm, of the open loop. The worked stitch has to be set down very carefully indeed if it is to hang symmetrically around the new loop.

Learning to make stitches which hang straight and not lop-sided is the only considerable challenge in hand-knitting.

Knitting machines are necessarily of fixed size and shape so the work must sometimes be adapted to them; they are usually too large and heavy to be easily portable.

Hand knitting tools are small and light, easily carried about by the knitter and are so adaptable that there is no limit to the possible size or shape of the work.

In machine knitting the fabric is fixed in position but the yarn can be moved freely from side to side.

In hand knitting the yarn has a fixed position in the hand but needles and fabric are moved from one hand to the other.

In machine knitting the yarn is laid from left to right across the fixed fabric when making one row and from right to left when making the next.

In hand knitting the yarn is kept in its position in the hand and the fabric is moved under it from the needle in the left hand to the needle in the right hand. All rows are worked in the same direction for the needles are taken into the opposite hands at the start of each row.

In machine knitting the yarn cannot be placed behind the work so bars can not be set down at the back nor can new loops be drawn to the front, so basically there is only one kind of stitch.

In hand knitting the yarn can be held at either back or front of the work so bars can be set down on either surface and new loops drawn either way, consequently there are two distinct kinds of stitch.

Machines can knit standard fabric with astonishing speed and evenness, but variations of fabric are neither as easily nor as quickly made as the plain fabric.

Hand knitting is slower than machine knitting but because every stitch is worked individually most of the many possible variations can be worked almost as fast as standard knit and purl.

Joining yarn invisibly

Joins in yarn are not inherently necessary. Many garments could be made from one continuous strand and yarn can be spun to a sufficient length for any piece of knitting. However, smaller units are more convenient to handle so knitters must learn to re-make a continuous strand. If done perfectly, the join would be neither felt nor seen, but, as slight imperfections are inevitable, joins should be kept away from edges and other places which get hard wear or which are decorative or conspicuous.

Before starting to make a join, find out how much yarn is needed to make half a dozen stitches. Work until at least that length of the ball of yarn remains unworked.

Figure 6 (opposite)   a   Unravel this ending tail into two parts, both, if possible with the same number of plies. Unravel the same length of the starting tail.
   b   Hold the tip of one part of the starting tail against the undivided part of the ending tail and make one stitch with all three parts.
   c   Keep hold of the plies of the starting tail and of that part of the ending tail which will together make up the original number of plies. Twist all the plies together in the original direction. Continue knitting with this twisted yarn.
   d   Hold the tip of the ending tail against the undivided part of the starting tail and make one stitch with all three parts.
   Continue knitting with the new ball. The spare plies show the area produced by one ball so keep them intact until their information can be of no further help.
   Always cut out any knot found within a ball and join the ends invisibly, cutting off the spare plies immediately.

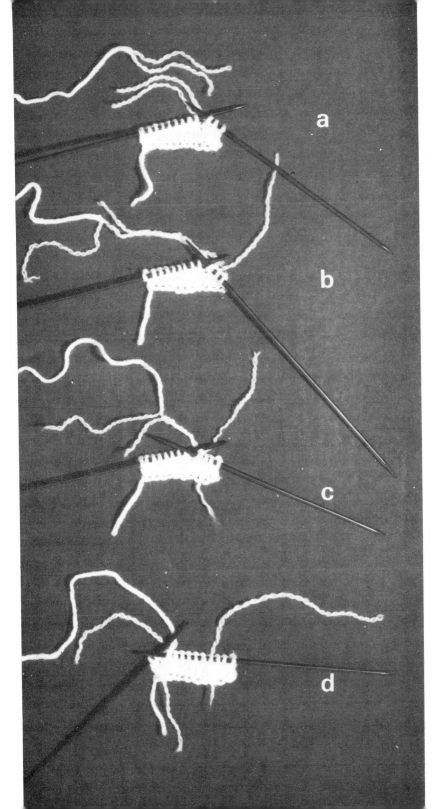

a

b

c

d

Knitting tools

The two essential components of a hand-knitting tool are a tapered tip for making stitches and a cylindrical shaft for holding them. Modern mass-produced knitting tools are excellent but are available in fewer lengths, thicknesses and materials than their earlier individually-made equivalents. The extra variety is often an asset so period tools should not be wantonly discarded.

Types of tool

A *knitting needle* consists of a shaft with a tip at each end. Needles can be used for almost every kind of knitting procedure. Needles are sold in sets. *Figure 7.*

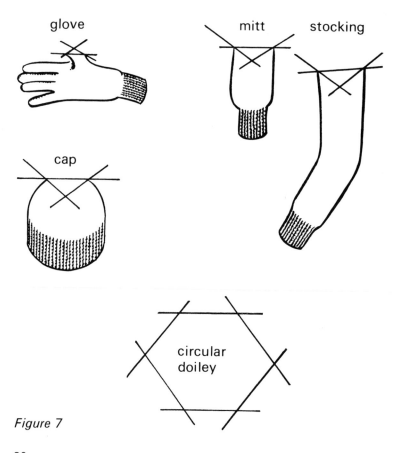

glove

mitt stocking

cap

circular doiley

Figure 7

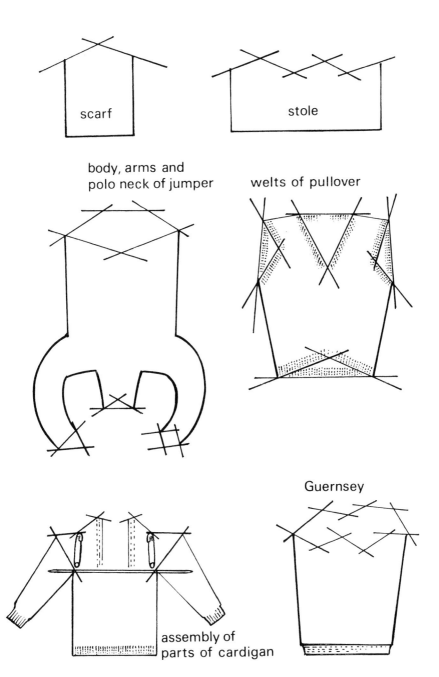

scarf

stole

body, arms and
polo neck of jumper

welts of pullover

assembly of
parts of cardigan

Guernsey

Figure 7 continued

A *circular needle* consists of a long flexible shaft with two stiffened tips forming a unit which is sold singly. Circular needles can be used for all kinds of knitting procedure except for making narrow tubes.

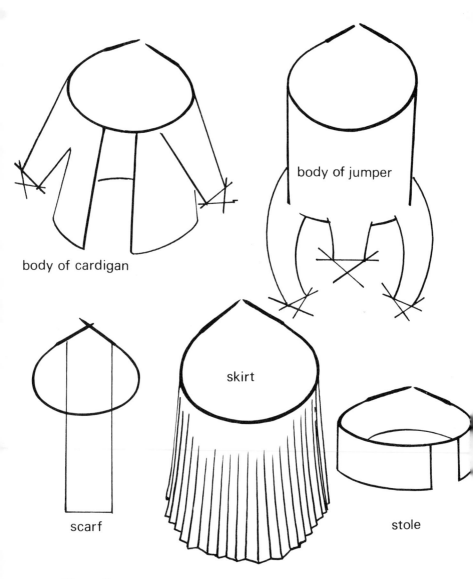

body of cardigan

body of jumper

scarf

skirt

stole

Figure 8

A *knitting pin* consists of a shaft with a tip at one end and a knob at the other. They are normally sold in pairs. Knitting pins can be used for making small, flat pieces, eg the vertically striped sleeve shown in *figure 9*, but they are of limited use.

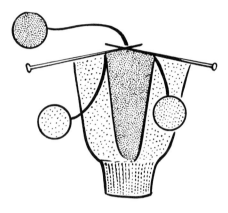

Figure 9

Materials

Wood is light and pleasant to use but is not strong enough for thin tools. *Plastic*, sometimes called bone, can be manufactured in so many colours that details of stitchmaking can always be made to show up clearly by the choice of a tool colour which contrasts with that of the yarn. Like wood, solid plastic can be cut and shaped if the only tools available are too long, or when needles are wanted but only pins can be found. The flexible part of a circular needle is always made of plastic though the ends are normally of metal. *Metal* is the only material really strong enough for the thin tools. It is most useful when it has a tinted surface or is covered with coloured plastic.

Thickness

The thickness of the shaft determines the size of the stitches moulded round it, which in turn affects the size of garments. This is so important that tools are numbered according to their thickness, irrespective of their length.

In the United Kingdom the higher the number the thinner the needle; in the USA the higher the number the thicker the needle; on the Continent of Europe thickness is measured directly in millimetres.

Comparative thicknesses

UK	14 13	12	11	10	9	8	7	6	5
USA	0 1		2	3	4	5	6	7	8 9
Metric	2 2½		3	3½	4		4½	5	

UK		4	3	2	1	0 00	000 0000
USA	10			10½		11	13	15
Metric	5½	6		6½ 7 7½		8	9	10

Tool sizes can be measured with a gauge pierced with numbered slots or holes into which the shaft (not the tip) must fit. The method of reading them should be tested by measuring a knitting pin which has its size marked permanently on its knob.

Tool lengths

Tool tips are steadiest and most fully under control when the upward pressure of the fingers exactly equals the downward pull of fabric and tool. The less these seem to weigh the less tired the supporting fingers will become.

When any stiff rod (such as a knitting pin) is supported at one end, a weight hanging from it will seem lighter when nearer the support than when further away.

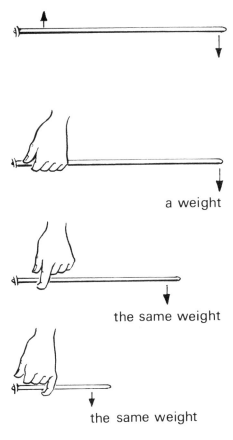

a weight

the same weight

the same weight

Figure 10

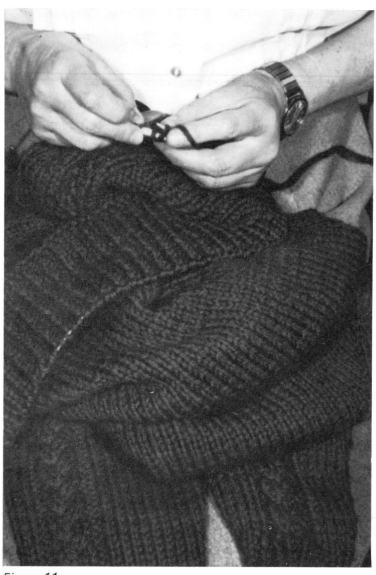

Figure 11

Knitting is generally least tiring when the weight of the work stays near or below the hands as when a circular needle is used. (*Figure 11*).

Professional knitters working with long stiff needles do not seem to tire because they wear knitting belts (*figure 12*) which carry almost all the weight. The use of these belts is not described in this book.

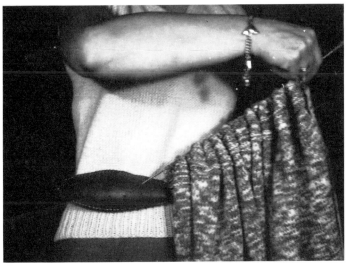

Figure 12

Tools which do not reach across the hand are even more tiring than those which project far beyond it. Knitters usually find that a needle just long enough to cross the hand diagonally (*figure 13*) is the most comfortable to use, whether or not it is joined to its fellow to make a circular needle.

Figure 13

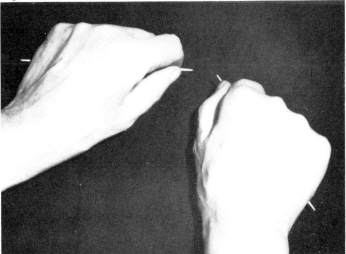

Labelling of digits

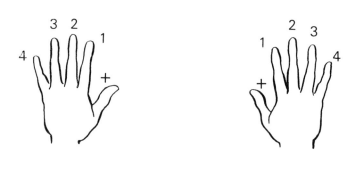

OR

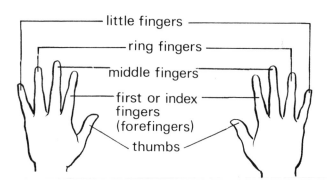

Figure 14

Holding the needles

Hold both needles in the same way, for they make the same movements, though at different times. Prepare to speed the work by sharing it between the needles, letting each go halfway toward the other, instead of making either of them move all the way on its own.

Hold the needles so that control over them is as complete as possible and so that each part of each hand can do its own particular job. Prepare for really rapid stitch-making by keeping the needle tips short and the finger tips close to them so that nothing has far to move. At first the beginner's need to see what is happening necessitates the wider spread of fingers and tips usually seen in illustrations.

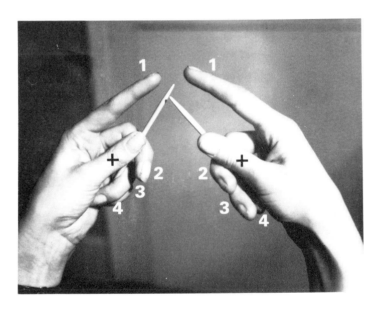

Figure 15

Thumbs press needles away. Middle fingers press needles forward. Ring fingers hold needles up against the palms and raise or lower them by varying the upward pressure. Little fingers, curled round the shaft of the needles, shift them lengthways.

Making a slip knot

All knitting starts with some kind of pre-formed loop, the most popular being the slip knot, which is easily tied and has much in common with the stitches used in knitting.

Figure 16a To make a slip knot, place the working end of the yarn across and just behind the basic loop within easy reach of the working needle. Press the needle tip from one surface of the basic loop to the other so that it can catch up the working end which is on that other surface. Draw the working end to the original surface.

b Pull the ends of the yarn. The new loop closes round the needle becoming the first stitch of the piece of knitting. It is ready to be taken into the left hand as the new 'pre-formed loop' or 'the stitch due to be worked next'.

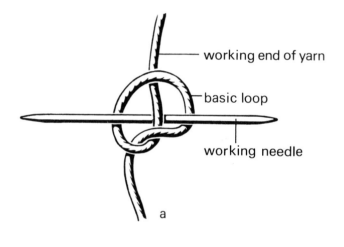

working end of yarn

basic loop

working needle

a

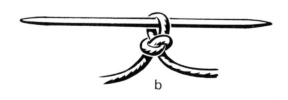

b

Figure 16

Holding the yarn

Almost all knitting is a repetition of the process of drawing the working end of yarn through a pre-formed loop. Normally, this loop is held on the tip of lhn (left hand needle) and the new loop made with the tip of the rhn (right hand needle) and kept on that tip so that the working end starts just below it.

Figure 17 In these positions the working end is most nearly in contact with the pre-formed loop if the yarn slopes up and to the left. Fortunately the left forefinger is available there to support it.

Figure 18 The right forefinger is less conveniently placed for holding the yarn but it can be used quite efficiently when tips and stitches are close together.

Figure 17

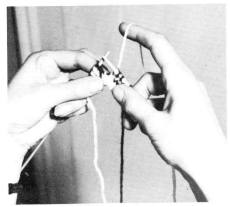

Figure 18

Figure 19 In more advanced knitting both forefingers are used at once for working two colours in the same row.

Figure 19

In these illustrations the working end is usually shown as rising vertically so that it suits all knitters equally.

Figures 20 and 21 During the making of bottom and side edges, the working end starts below the left needle, not the right. This makes the yarn slope awkwardly enough to slow the work slightly but there are so few of these stitches that it is not necessary to use a different method for them.

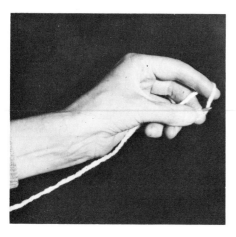

Figure 20

Figure 21

Figure 22   Yarn must be kept under control by the fingers. The grip must be potentially strong but the simpler the arrangement of the yarn the less time is lost in getting work re-started.

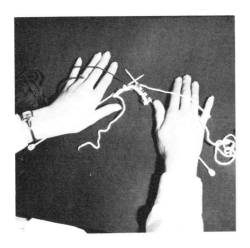

Figure 22

Casting on by the simple method

Casting on is the process of making the first row of stitches, starting with the slip knot. This row is different from all others in having no stitches beneath it. Being different, it has a special name—the cast-on row.

Not all ways of casting on look the same when finished. Later on, knitters should learn how to produce different effects by using other methods. The *simple method* is best for learners because its movements are used in other manipulations.

Figure 23a Use the left thumb and middle finger to open the slip knot just enough to admit the tip of rhn.

b *Press rhn far enough through the space to catch up the working end of yarn.

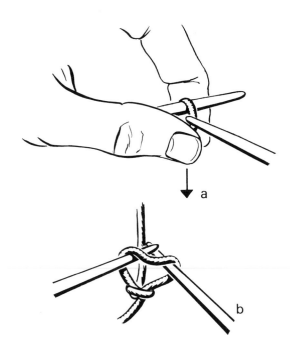

Figure 23

c Draw the working end forward as (*d*) a new stitch, held on rhn.

e Bring the tip of lhn to the right of the new stitch, then into it. As usual, the second tip in a stitch must go below the one already there.

f Move rhn below lhn. There are two stitches on lhn. Rhn is ready for a repetition of these movements.*

g Repeat until lhn holds the number of stitches specified.

Asterisks in knitting patterns indicate that the part between the similar signs is to be repeated.

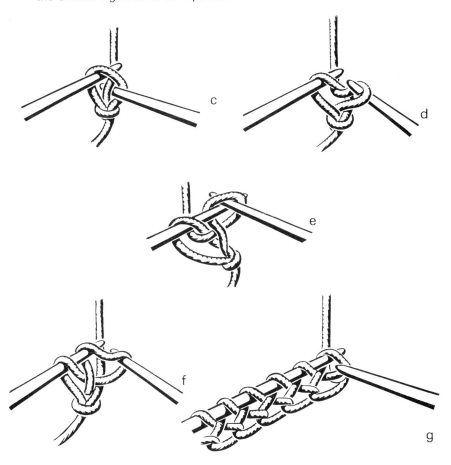

Figure 23
continued

Casting on in preparation for making a tube

Casting on, on a circular needle

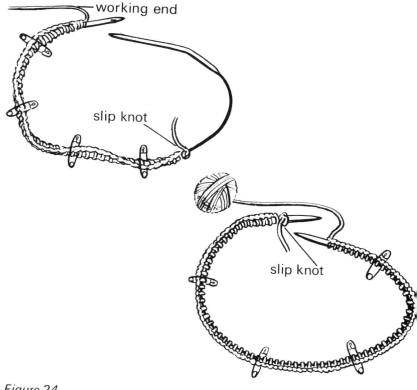

Figure 24

Complete the cast-on row. Fasten small safety pins around the linking parts of every twenty-fourth stitch to make counting easier.

Draw the slip knot to the tip of the needle. Take it into the left hand and the other tip into the right hand all ready to make a knit stitch.

Tight cast-on edges can be disastrous. To avoid making a sock edge too tight to go over the heel or a polo collar which will not go over the head, cast on to needles two or more sizes thicker than those to be used for the fabric.

Casting on, on a set of needles

Cast on to Needle 1 the stipulated number of stitches. Keep the next loop on Needle 2. Take Needle 2 into the left hand. It becomes lhn. Cast on to Needle 2 the stipulated number of stitches. Repeat this on Needle 3.

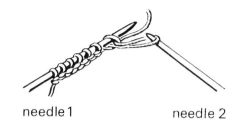

needle 1   needle 2

Draw the slip knot to the tip of its needle. Take that needle into the left hand as lhn. Take the empty needle into the right hand as rhn, all ready to make a knit stitch.

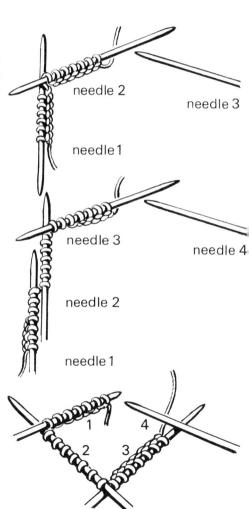

Figure 25

Making a knit stitch

A *knit* stitch is a loop drawn to the front of the work under a bar which is set down behind it.

Figure 26a Get into the knit position, ie with the yarn at the back of the work, tip of lhn above and slightly behind rhn, and tip of rhn leaning back against the front arm of the stitch at the tip of lhn, but not splitting the yarn.

b Insert rhn knitwise into the stitch, ie draw lhn forward and press rhn away so that the tip of rhn slides through the loop and under lhn until it is just behind the working end of yarn.

c Make the knit stitch, ie press lhn away and draw rhn forward until the new loop emerges at the front through the original stitch.

d Set down the *knitted* stitch, ie place the bar of the knitted stitch exactly *behind* the centre of the new knit stitch and use the little finger of the left hand to withdraw lhn from the *knitted* stitch. Make sure that the new knit stitch slopes correctly from upper left to lower right across rhn when the row is spread out along the needle.

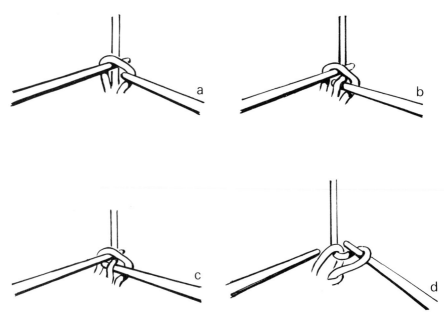

Figure 26

Making a purl stitch

A *purl* stitch is a loop drawn to the back of the work under a bar which is set down in front of it.

Figure 27a Get into the purl position, ie with the yarn at the front of the work, tip of lhn above rhn, and tip of rhn leaning forward against the front arm of the stitch.

b Insert rhn purlwise into the stitch, ie press lhn away and draw rhn forward so that the tip of rhn slides through the stitch, under and in front of lhn, but stays behind the working end of yarn.

c Twist yarn and needle together by moving the yarn and the tip of rhn in small circles in opposite directions to make one complete turn of yarn around rhn.

When the movement is familiar a purl stitch will remain on the tip even if this is quite short. Try to keep the tips short to avoid wasting time and effort.

d Make the purl stitch, ie draw lhn forward and press rhn away until the new loop emerges at the back through the original stitch.

e Set down the *purled* stitch, ie place the bar of the purled stitch exactly *in front of* the centre of the new purl stitch, and use the little finger of the left hand to withdraw lhn from the purled stitch. Make sure that the new purl stitch slopes correctly from upper left to lower right across rhn.

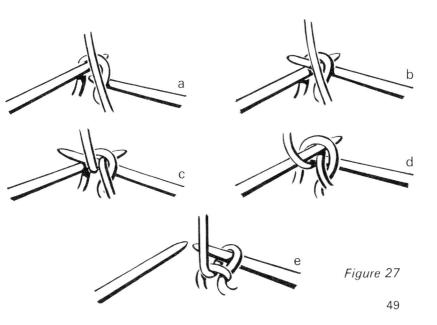

Figure 27

Making simple ribbing

Ribbing consists of alternate knit and purl columns.
Figure 28a   Get yarn and needles into the knit position.

b   *Complete a knit stitch.

c   Move yarn and needles to the purl position.

d   Complete a purl stitch.

e   Move yarn and needles to the knit position.*

Continue like this, working the first round or row.

When a circular needle is being used, continue as far as the end of the round or row. When knitting needles or pins are being used, continue until lhn is empty.

Advantages of ribbing as a beginner's first fabric

Both basic movements are encountered within the first two stitches and the two movements are given equal emphasis and practice. The nature of knit and purl as obverse and reverse is emphasised. Appearance is the best guide to the rhythm of the work, for the learner soon realises that the knit stitches are made above knit columns and purl stitches at the top of purl columns. Mistakes show up clearly, encouraging both accuracy and immediate correction. Many simple garments can be made entirely from ribbing and indeed, most knitted garments start with it.

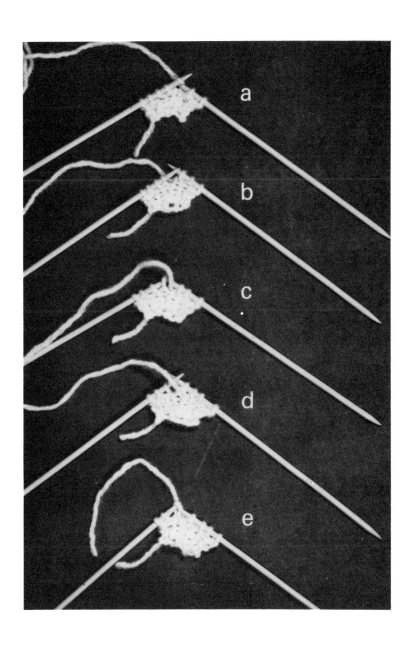

Figure 28

51

Starting on the next needle

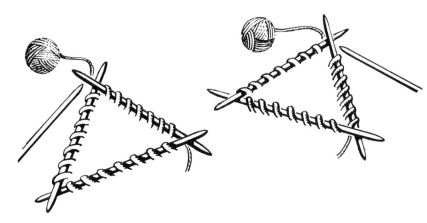

Figure 29

When lhn is empty change needles to make a fresh set of stitches available for working.

When working in rounds (*figure 29*) *take the emptied needle into the right hand. It becomes rhn. Take the next needle of the round into the left hand. It becomes lhn. Work across lhn until it is empty.*

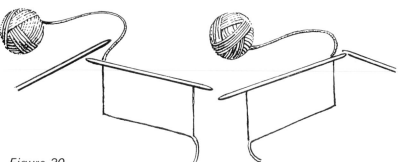

Figure 30

When working in rows (*figure 30*) *take the emptied needle in the right hand as rhn. Take the knitting on its needle into the left hand. That needle becomes lhn. Work across lhn.*

Starting a second round

The loops on the needle are less bulky than the linking part below so, when close-packed, a cast-on round often gets twisted (*figure 31a*). Spread out the work, untwist it and arrange the linking part outside the ring (or triangle) of needles (*b*). Be sure that not one twist remains. Make one stitch. Permanent twisting is now impossible, and continuous work will produce a simple tube (*c*).

Figure 31d Work which resembles what mathematicians call a *Möbius strip* had one twist left at the start of round 2. It will never become a simple tube.

Make use of the working of the ribbed tube to practise:
  Setting down the bar of the worked stitch correctly in the centre of the column of stitches.
  Making both hands and all fingers co-operate.
  Reducing general muscular tension.
  Achieving regularity both of movement and of tension on the yarn.
  Keeping every stitch intact and never splitting yarn.
  Maintaining the rhythm by inspection and touch rather than stitch counting.
  Working more and more rapidly.

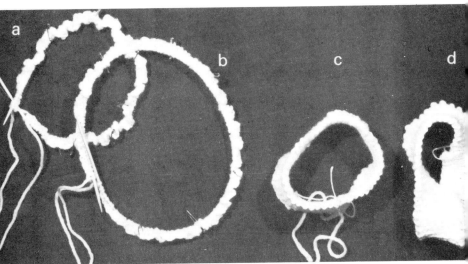

Figure 31

Junction of rounds

Figure 32a   There is always a small step and a gap between the end and the beginning of a cast-on round. Eventually these will be stitched over but they can never be completely hidden and (*b*) there is necessarily a step between the last and the first stitches of any round, so column 1 is usually allocated to the least conspicuous part of the garment.

c   On the first round, the first stitch is made into the slip knot; in all later rounds, the first stitch is made into the column above the slip knot. The first stitch of a round can always be found by tracking up the column above the starting tail, but it can be identified more promptly if column 1 is kept marked with safetypins.

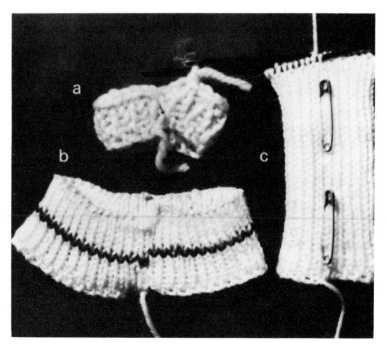

Figure 32

Good stitch making

Stitches are most likely to be centred correctly if this stringent, yet simple, test is regularly applied.

Use spare thick yarn and a set of short needles. Cast on 24 stitches. Join the row into a ring. Work in rib for six rounds. Change from rounds to rows; ie having reached the end of a round, turn and work back along the needle just worked, keeping to the established ridges. Continue as far as column 1, then again turn and work 24 stitches. Work to and fro for six rows. A vertical gap will form. Work several bands of rounds and rows alternately.

Figure 33a shows clearly that all stitches have been correctly centred, whereas *b* demonstrates the result of working the stitches lop-sided.

'Work' is used as a specific instruction when it is impossible to know, or unnecessary to state exactly how many stitches or rows are involved, or which are knit and which purl.

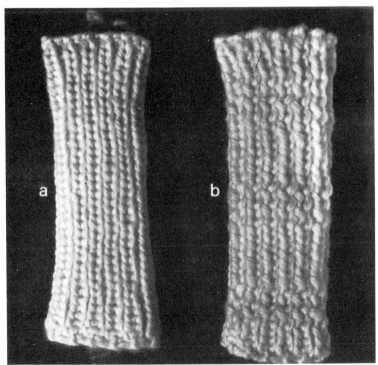

Figure 33

Good round making

All columns of a tube should be evenly spaced (*figure 34a*). With circular needles there should be no difficulty in this but with sets of needles the interruption which is inevitable at every change of needle could (*b*) spoil the shape of the tube so, for a few stitches before and after the needle-break, modify the tension; ie change the pull on the yarn sufficiently to ensure complete regularity of fabric.

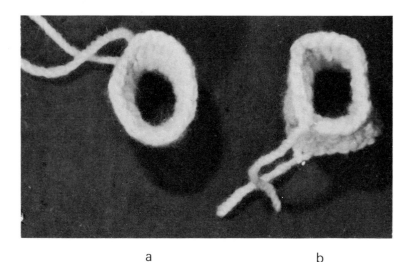

a   b

Figure 34

Protecting knitting

To protect the knitting, keep it in a paper or plastic bag of suitable size, with the needles and top few rows protruding. A rubber band around its neck will keep everything in position.

Dropped stitches, ladders and picked up stitches

Stitches may be dropped purposely, either permanently to make openwork fabric; or temporarily to give access to a mistake or to join side edges. If dropped accidentally they will form ladders which tend to run quickly if the yarn is slippery, like nylon, but if the surface of the yarn is rough and hairy, like mohair, the ladder may not start to form unless the work is pulled. A stitch can not start to ladder when it is held by another stitch, a knitting tool, a strand of yarn, a crochet hook or safetypin.

Figure 35 A stitch which is free to do so always nods its head towards the knit surface of the stitch below. A safetypin will prevent a stitch from laddering further. A crochet hook is useful in picking up dropped stitches. The hook could be inserted into either surface of the dropped stitch. The surface it enters becomes the knit surface of that stitch.

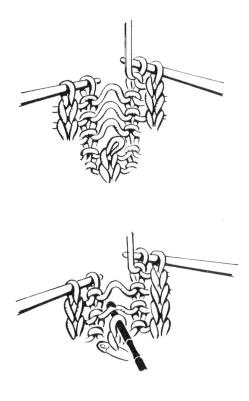

Figure 35

The language of knitting patterns

Most knitting patterns are conveniently and economically short, kept so by the use of abbreviations and the omission of all inessential details. Knitters must master the language as well as the techniques of the craft if they are to follow patterns successfully.

Abbreviations

As might be expected, technical terms are usually represented by their initial letters (K, P and W for knit, purl and work) but the practice is plagued with anomalies:

1 the use or omission of full stops and the use of capitals or lower case letters is capricious.

2 initials only are used habitually when they refer to the number of stitches to be worked (K2, P6, W12) but more erratically in reference to other units (K 4 rows, P 6 rounds, W 12 repeats).

3 in traditional groupings, the meanings may be quite different. In 'psso'; the 'p' means 'pass', one 's' means 'slip', the other means 'stitch' and the 'o' means 'over'.

4 the many knitting terms which start with 's' may be distinguished by the use of a second letter, but this often depends upon the other terms used in that set of instructions. 'Stitch' may be printed as 's' or 'st' and 'slip' as 's' or 'sl', so confusion can easily arise between 'sl 2' and 's 12'.

In addition, some words are represented by their first syllable so, not surprisingly, every set of knitting instructions includes a list of the abbreviations it uses. Those used in this book are given on page 153.

Terminology

Traditional wording is often ambiguous but rarely confusing.

The word 'stitch', for example, means either the constituent loops of a fabric or the fabric itself, as in 'stocking stitch' (ambiguously abbreviated to 'st st').

The word 'plain' as a synonym for 'knit' is rarely used in print.

Symbols

The commonest symbol is the repeat sign, usually one asterisk placed before the instructions to be repeated, and another after them, eg *K1 P1*. The number of the repeats may be given first (Rounds 1 – 18 *K1 P1*), or after the second asterisk (*K1 P1* for 18 rounds).

Brackets or double asterisks may also be used as repeat signs when groups of stitches alternate with others. More than one type may appear in a complex instruction.

The layout of knitting patterns

Knitting patterns planned for *continuous narrative* as on page 144 are sometimes arranged with the numbers in columns:

Cast on	148
st as a tube. Work	18
rounds in rib. Change to No. 9 needles and work	3
rounds in st st . . .	

Both forms are simple to read but both necessarily start at the top and work down, whereas knitting actually starts at the bottom and works up, so knitters do not find either layout ideal.

Box diagrams on the other hand, are deliberately designed to suit knitters' needs, for they start at the bottom and progress upward to allow direct comparison with the work; they show how many stitches there should be at any stage; they give a running total of complete rows worked and they often indicate the shape of the garment.

The box diagram on pages 146 and 147 gives the same instructions as pages 144 and 145. The first box, ie the box at the bottom of page 146 reads

```
1 ——————— 148 ┌─────────────────────────────┐
                │ Cast on                     │
0 ———————    0 └─────────────────────────────┘
```

This shows that at the start there are neither rows nor stitches, but that after the first (cast-on) row, there should be 148 stitches. The second box, immediately above the first and sharing some of its data, reads

```
19 ——————— 148 ┌─────────────────────────────┐
                │ *K1 P1* as tube             │
1 ——————— 148  └─────────────────────────────┘
```

showing that 18 rows of rib must be worked next and that the number of stitches must stay the same. Progressing upward, the other boxes are read similarly, those without sides giving instructions for re-arrangements.

Several *sizes of garment* may be given in any one leaflet, for usually each differs from others of the same shape only in the numbers of rows and of columns. The numbers sometimes seem erratic but those relevant to the smallest size always come first, then the rest in increasing order of garment size. If one number only is given it applies to all sizes. If there is fear of confusion, unwanted numbers can be pencilled out.

If the pullover pattern were printed in two sizes, it might start

'Cast on 148 (150) st as a tube. Work 18 (22) rounds in rib . . .'

or, if set out in tabular form as

Cast on	148	150
st as a tube. Work	18	22
rounds in rib. Change to No. 9 needles		
and work	3	3
rounds in st st . . .		

The box diagram would begin

```
19(23)-148 (150) ┌─────────────────────────────┐
                  │ *K1 P1* as tube             │
1 (1) -148 (150)  ├─────────────────────────────┤
                  │ Cast on                     │
0 (0) -  0  (0)   └─────────────────────────────┘
```

Counting rows or rounds

Different pattern leaflets have different ways of showing the number of rounds or rows to be worked.

1   All are numbered consecutively from start to finish.
2   The cast-on row is excluded from the numbering, and some-times others, also, are excluded.
3   Numbering is started afresh at each change of fabric.

In any fabric, the first round or row to be worked is called the bottom row, even in garments which progress toward the feet from neck or waist.

Figure 36   To make the count use a short knitting needle as a pointer; rest its tip in the first row of the fabric; move the pointer up the column in step with the counting, and include in the total the row on the needle.

When counting rows, check the result by noticing the posi-tion of the starting and ending tails. If they are above one another the total number of rows, including the cast on, must be even.

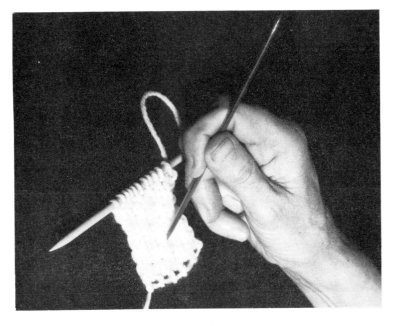

Figure 36

Figure 37a When counting rounds, the tails do not show whether the number is odd or even but do show whether the round has been completed. Allow for this when selecting the column to be counted.

   b Keep count by fastening a small safetypin into three or four stitches of the twelfth and each succeeding twelfth round or row.

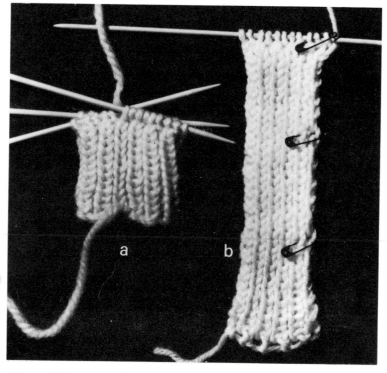

Figure 37

†

Varieties of knitted fabrics

Ribbing, stocking stitch and reversed stocking stitch are just three of the three hundred or more fabrics encountered in knitting leaflets. A stock of samplers of the fabrics should be available for study in every handicraft room or knitting cupboard. If possible they should be fixed in a card index or album in such a way that they show whether both surfaces can be used as 'right' sides; all made of the same springy wool to demonstrate texture; all made on the same thickness of tool for general comparison; and all with the same number of rows and columns for comparison of area, stitch size and stitch shape. Ideally, the samplers should consist of 26 rows altogether and 26 columns so that the outside stitches form a frame and the fabric is made on the central 24 columns and rows, which will accommodate the most popular repeats of 2, 3, 4, 6 and 8. Comments, such as notes on ease of working and of the differences between the working of rounds and of rows, should be added as knowledge is gained. Examples given on the next few pages suggest some uses of the samplers at different stages of a knitter's career from its start, when the beginner needs to be sure of the appearance of the fabric she is trying to master, to its culmination, when the accomplished knitter utilises different stitch shapes and sizes for subtle garment tailoring, while combining their appearance into interesting effects.

An examination of simple ribbing

Abbreviation Rib.

Instruction *K1 P1* on rounds or rows with an even number of stitches.

Characteristics (figure 38) *a* It does not curl. Both surfaces look the same, show knit stitches only, and are vertically ridged. It feels thick and looks narrow but can be pulled wider.

b When pulled wider it feels thinner and purl columns appear between the knit ridges. When it is released it becomes narrow again, feels thick again and purl columns recede once more.

c When off the needle the stitches are seen to be pushed forward by the bars behind them so that alternate columns lie almost in front of their neighbours, making the fabric seem narrow and thick, and the bars linking the back-to-back columns are short.

d When ribbing is pulled out sideways the linking bars are made longer and the alternate purl columns can be seen. Also, the linking bars are made to curve if the fabric is pulled sideways. If the yarn is springy the bars resist this deformation, giving the elasticity which is characteristic of true ribbing. If the yarn is obedient, not springy, the bars remain curved and there is less elasticity.

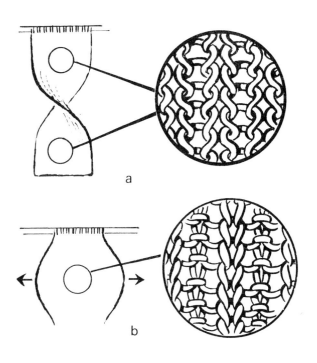

a

b

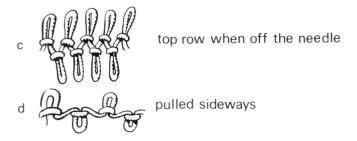

c   top row when off the needle

d   pulled sideways

Figure 38

An examination of garter stitch

This fabric seems conspicuously different from ribbing, yet has much in common with it.

Abbreviations   Gs, g st, etc.

Instructions   Rounds: round 1, knit; round 2, purl.
Rows: all knit, or all purl.

Similarities between ribbing and garter stitch   Both are free from curl and have two surfaces which look alike. The fabric produced feels thick and is stiff along the ridges. It is also springy between the ridges, revealing the other kind of stitch.

Differences between ribbing and garter stitch   Ribbing is tall and narrow, with stiff ridges running vertically and is apparently made of knit stitches. The fabric produced is springy horizontally and is easily arranged so that the ridges cling at waist and cuffs.

Garter stitch is wide and shallow, with stiff ridges running horizontally and is apparently made of purl stitches. The fabric produced is springy vertically and is not easily arranged so that the ridges cling at waist and cuffs.

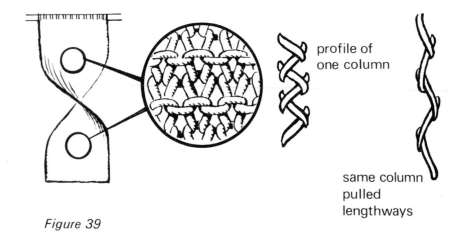

profile of
one column

same column
pulled
lengthways

Figure 39

An examination of moss stitch

This fabric has much in common with garter stitch.

Abbreviation   Ms, M st etc.

Instruction   *K1 P1* on rounds or rows with an odd number of stitches.

Similarities between moss stitch and garter stitch   Both are free from curl and have two surfaces which look alike, mainly consisting of the bars of purl stitches. Both feel thicker than stocking stitch and are shallow but can be pulled taller, and are wide and can not easily be pulled wider. Both can be used for making into whole garments or for edging tailored garments of stocking stitch.

Differences between moss stitch and garter stitch   Garter stitch is shallow and feels thick. Its bars are arranged in ridges and though it is stiff along the ridges it is springy across them.

Moss stitch is only fairly shallow, feels only fairly thick and is only fairly springy in either direction, its bars being arranged in a lattice.

Each column of moss stitch is identical with any column of garter stitch so they are often interchangeable, but moss stitch is slightly stiffer and taller because its adjacent columns are reversed, stiffening the linking bars. It is less rapidly worked than garter stitch because the yarn must be shifted more often.

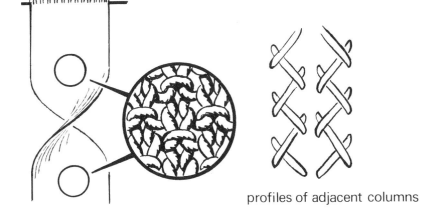

profiles of adjacent columns

Figure 40

An examination of stocking stitch and reverse stocking stitch

This is also called knit fabric and purl fabric.

Abbreviations   St st, st st, etc.

Instructions   Rounds: all knit (or all purl, which gives purl fabric outside the tube and stocking stitch within). Rows: row 1, knit. row 2, purl.

Stocking stitch, made entirely of the vertically overlapping arms of knit stitches is the smoothest fabric at the knitter's command. Figure *41*a.

Reverse stocking stitch is not quite as smooth. It consists entirely of horizontally arranged bars. *Figure 41b.*

Stocking stitch tends to curl so all garments made in it must have some kind of welt at every edge. Both its surfaces can be greatly, and often unexpectedly, changed by variations of the colour or the spin of the yarn.

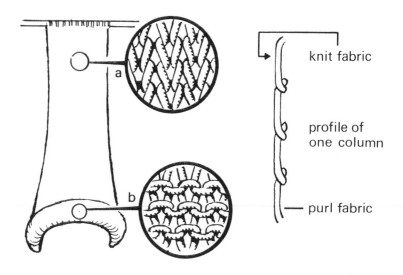

knit fabric

profile of
one column

purl fabric

Figure 41

Effect of yarn tension on the regularity of stitches

Knitters' fingers do two jobs simultaneously.
1   They manipulate the needles to make knit and purl stitches.
2   They control the flow of yarn. When they let it run loosely the stitches are large, when they grip it tightly the stitches are small.

If work is to look regular, tension on the yarn must be kept constant, even when the kind of stitch is changed. If the tension is not constant the two kinds of stitch will not be the same size. The difference shows most clearly in purl fabric pulled length-ways. In *figure 42*, the fabric on the left shows the effect of knit stitches worked at the *same* tension as purl stitches; the fabric on the right shows the effect of knit stitches worked at a *different* tension from purl stitches.

Figure 42

Stitch size

The patchwork blankets valued by charities are often group efforts, all members being told to 'work in gs, using DK. wool and No. 8 tools. Cast on 3 st. Add 1 st at beg. of each row to 40 st. Rem. 1 st at beg. of each row to 3 st. Cast off.'

The resultant squares may vary greatly in size, for some knitters grip yarn tightly so their stitches, and their squares, are small; others maintain little tension on their yarn so their stitches, and squares, are large. Yet all expect that a garment they make from a printed pattern will be the specified size. This can only be so if the stitches are the size specified in the pattern, so before any garment is started, stitch size should be tested. (Beginners need not worry if they have made ribbing without having done this.)

Making and using a stitch size sampler

Needles and yarn   Use those named in the pattern.

Fabric   Unless otherwise instructed, use stocking stitch even when it does not appear in the pattern. No other simple fabric is inelastic enough to give reliable results.

Size   Use enough stitches to give a total width of about 6 in. (150 mm) so that the flat part is at least 4 or 5 in. (100 or 125 mm) wide to lessen the inaccuracy caused by difficulty in estimating fractions of a stitch. Both $5\frac{3}{4}$ and $6\frac{1}{4}$ stitches look much like 6 if measured over 1 in. (25 mm) only. However, these variations could make a difference of 3 in. (76 mm) in a garment planned to be 36 in. (92 cm) wide when worked at 6 stitches per inch. The inaccuracy of a quarter of a stitch in 4 or 5 in. (100 or 125 mm) produces a variation of little more than $\frac{1}{2}$ in. (15 mm) in the 36 in. (92 cm) garment.

Measurement   Fasten a pin between columns near one edge of the flat part. Place a ruler with an inch (or cm) mark exactly over the pin. Fasten another pin near the other edge of the flat fabric where a column edge coincides with another inch (or cm) mark. Count the columns between the pins and note their distance apart. Calculate the stitch size in columns (or stitches) in an inch. (Metric results are expressed in whatever unit is most convenient, possibly 13 stitches in 5 cm, or 11 st in 4 cm or even 9 st in 3 cm. The number in a single centimetre is too small for accuracy.) If the stitches are the specified size, the garment also should be the specified size.

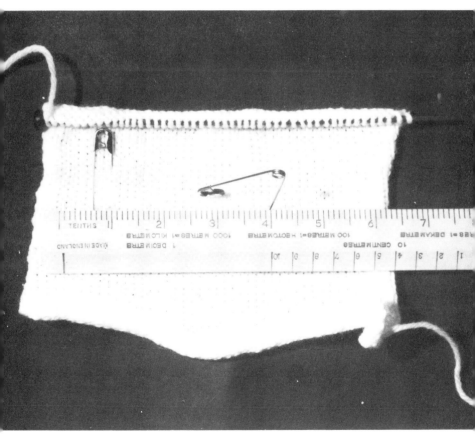

Figure 43

Two ways of changing stitch size

If the stitches of the sampler are the wrong size they must be changed, or the garment will be the wrong size. Two ways of making the change are illustrated (*figure 44*).

Effects of variations of yarn tension (top row)
These three stitch-size samplers were made with the same yarn and needles and in exact accordance with the instructions yet their sizes differ.

   a has the stipulated stitch size for it was worked at the expected tension;

   b has smaller stitches than stipulated for it was worked with the yarn held too tightly, ie at high tension;

   c has larger stitches than stipulated for it was worked with the yarn held slack, ie at low tension.

Very few knitters can deliberately modify their habitual tension accurately enough to be sure that the garment will be the size planned.

Effects of variations of needle thickness (middle row)
These three samplers were worked at the same tension in the same yarn and with the same number of columns and rows, but a different thickness of needle was used for each.

   d has the stipulated stitch size for the needles were the stipulated size (and the yarn was kept at the expected tension);

   e has larger stitches than *a* because thicker needles were used;

   f has smaller stitches than *a* because thinner needles were used.

Almost all knitters who need to alter their stitch size do so by changing their needle size.

Using needle thickness to counteract tension variations (bottom row)
These three samplers all have stitches of the same size but

   g was worked at the expected tension on needles of the stipulated size;

   h was worked at the same high tension as *b* but on the thick needles used for *e*;

   i was worked at the same low tension as *c* but on the thin needles used for *f*.

   If the first sampler does not produce the stipulated stitch size, make others, using needles of different thickness, until the correct stitch size is produced. Substitute the one needle size for the other throughout the pattern.

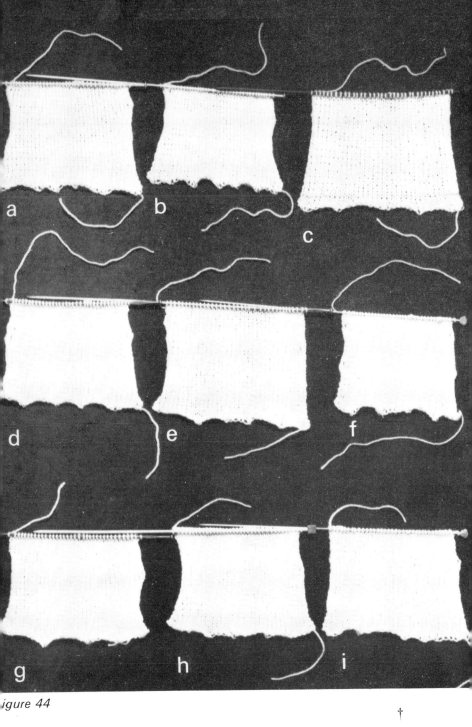

a b c
d e f
g h i

Figure 44

Some basic ways of shaping

The methods used in shaping knitted fabric are generally worked symmetrically and are illustrated in *figure 45*.

- *a*   changing the number of stitches in the row
- *b*   changing the number of stitches in the column
- *c*   changing the needle size and therefore the stitch size
- *d*   changing the fabric and therefore the stitch shape
- *e*   changing the direction of the work.

Figure 45

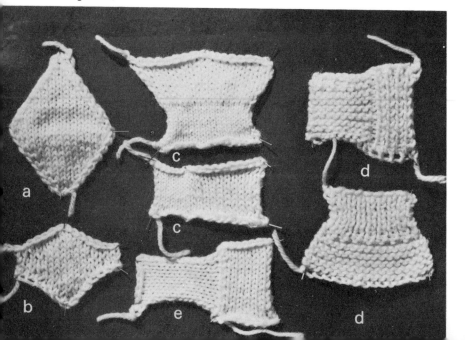

Some ways of shaping tubes

All methods may be, and usually are, symmetrical. *Figure 46* shows tubes shaped by using darts (D), gussets (G) and gathers (Ga) or by making different pieces of fabric seem continuous, even if worked in different directions (C).

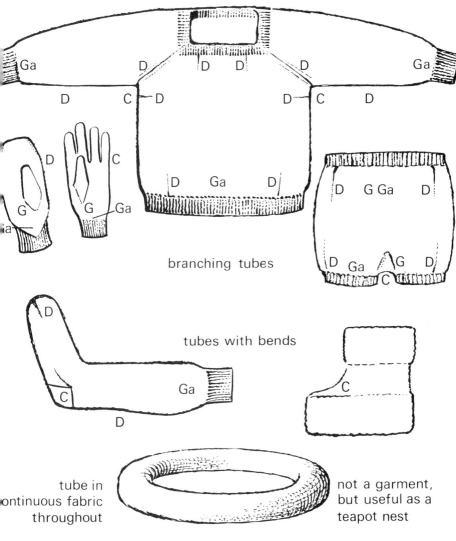

branching tubes

tubes with bends

tube in
ontinuous fabric
throughout

not a garment,
but useful as a
teapot nest

Figure 46

Stitch shape

Figure 47a shows that individual stitches are circular while on needles but when worked are pear-shaped and seem to occupy a square of space. Nevertheless (*b*) because rows must over-lap and columns need not, a patch of stocking stitch with the same number of rows as of columns is not square, but oblong.

Figure 48 shows that the exact shape of the oblong may be affected by (*a*) the relative thickness of yarn and needles, (*b*) by the type of yarn, especially its stiffness and particularly (*c*) by the fabric.

Pattern leaflets make sure the garment will be the expected length as well as width by stipulating the number of rows as well as of columns in an inch (or in a specified number of centimetres).

The proportions of a garment depend upon the stitch size and shape so its dimensions should be determined entirely by column or row counting. Knitted pieces can be pulled temporarily out of shape so, though measurements can give rough guides to the amount of work done, the final decision should be based entirely on counting.

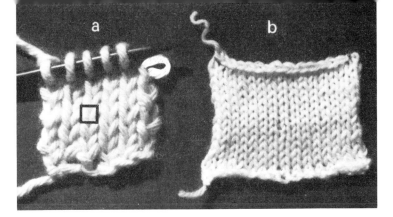

Figure 47

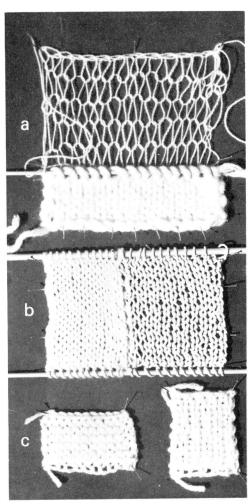

Figure 48

Some implications of stitch shape

Knitting patterns drawn on squared paper must be treated with great caution if they are being made up in any fabric where stitches behave as if they were oblong.

Squares can be knitted in stocking stitch but they must have more rows than columns.

When squares are set out diagonally on squared paper and each space is treated as a knit stitch, they turn into a set of diamonds as in Argyle socks, where the diamonds are worked in different colours. If the colour is changed on every row the diamonds are squat but they are tall when the change is made on alternate rows.

If correctly proportioned patterns are drawn on squared paper but no allowance is made for stitch shape, the finished garments will not be in proportion.

Different fabrics may have very different average stitch shapes, as shown by the tall, narrow shape of rib compared with the wide, shallow shape of garter stitch. A garment will look ludicrous if worked in one stitch shape, though planned for a fabric of a very different stitch shape.

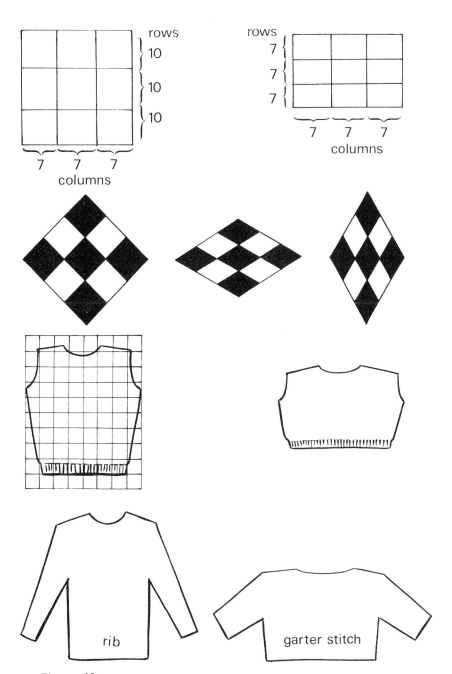

Figure 49

Adding a stitch by lifting the linking bar

This may be done in either of two symmetrical ways.

Lift the linking bar on to the tip of lhn. It becomes a bar and two arms. In one method *Figure 50*, the left arm is behind lhn. In the other (*b*), it is in front of it. Work a stitch around the left arm of the linking bar. Set down the worked bar.

The use of the left arm instead of the right twists the bar, preventing the formation of a hole.

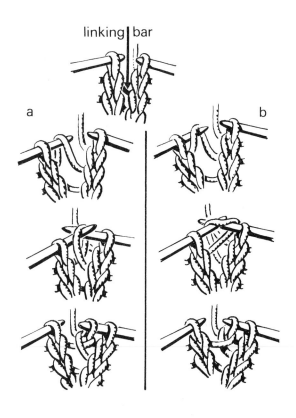

Figure 50

Adding a stitch by lifting the bar of a worked stitch

There are two symmetrical methods. In both, repeated lifting of the same bar strains the yarn.

Figure 51a   Lift the bar of the next worked stitch, ie the bar below the loop at the tip of lhn. Place it on the tip of lhn. Work the lifted bar, taking care not to involve the unworked stitch within it. Set down the doubly worked bar. Continue normally.

To work its pair (*b*), lift the bar from the column just worked. It is not, this time, the bar immediately below the open loop but the bar below that, ie belonging to the same row as the bar lifted in the symmetrical addition. Place the bar on lhn. Work it. Set it down. Continue working.

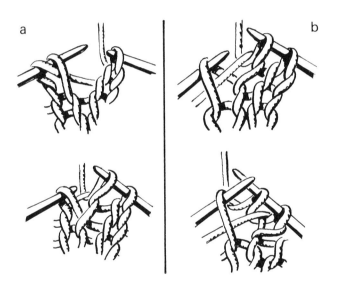

Figure 51

In printed patterns the instruction rows which involve the addition (or removal) of stitches often end with a number, alone, in brackets. This number indicates how many stitches should be on the needle when that row has been worked.

Shaping by adding stitches

Making a gusset as at the thumb of a glove

Choose the approximate position of the thumb to bring Column 1 of the welt to the front of the wrist. *Figure 52* shows a right hand glove. Mark the outlines of the thumb gusset by fastening pins in to two columns arising from knit ridges (for appearance sake) and separated by one or more columns (to reduce strain on the yarn).

Figure 53   Add stitches symmetrically on every 4th round, each just within an outline column.

Making darts as under the bust of women's garments

Allocate Column 1 to an underarm, preferably the left.
   Figure 54   Mark columns in the approximate lines of bust prominence. Each marked column will become the centre of the spine of a dart.

Figure 55   On every 4th round add two stitches symmetrically just outside the spine to make the dart.
   In sleeves, and wherever the first column of the round is part of the spine of the dart, add the first stitch near the end of a round and the second stitch near the start of the next round, so that the shapings will seem level.

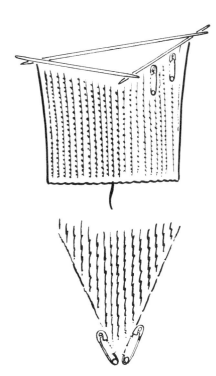

Figure 52

Figure 53

Figure 54

Figure 55

†

83

Shaping by working parts of rows

A line diagram is a convenient way of showing which parts of any rows are to be left unworked.

A semi-mitre in a strip of ribbing (*figure 56a*)   Work across all the stitches. Work all the stitches except the last two. Turn (ie change needles, even though both hold stitches). *Work to the end of the row. Work all stitches except the last two of the previous row. Turn.*

Completing the mitre (*b*)   Having worked the semi-mitre, work back. Work 2 stitches. Turn. Work back. Work 4 stitches. Turn. Work back. Work two more stitches on each row until all are included.

A dutch heel in a sock (*c*)   Work in knit fabric on half the stitches of the round. Mark them off into three symmetrical groups. Work across all except the last stitch. Turn. Work the next row similarly. *Work all except the last stitch of the previous row. Turn.*
Continue until the middle group only, is worked. *Work across the previous row and one stitch more. Turn.* Repeat until all the stitches are again being worked.

Dotted lines in a line diagram indicate that columns are continued later.

Preventing holes at turns (*figure 57*)   Before turning, slip the next loop off lhn; bring the yarn around the loop; return the loop to lhn then turn.
When, eventually, this loop is due to be worked, put the tip of rhn under the bend of yarn; then through the loop and over the other part of the bend. Finish the stitch normally. The bend will not be seen on the knit surface.

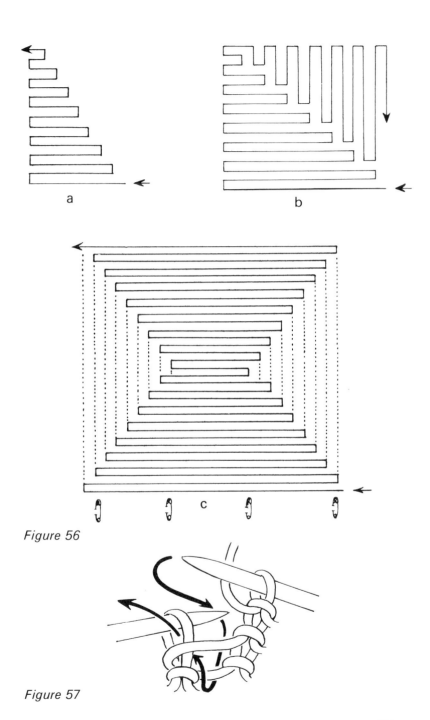

Figure 56

Figure 57

Making sloping rows

These are often used when completing the back of a cardigan or jumper.

Figure 58 Mark off the shoulders from the back of the neck. Mark off each shoulder into four equal groups of stitches. Work to and fro, ending each of the progressively shorter lines at a marked column.

Each turn shows as a slight step, separated from the next by several columns. Work at least two rows across all the turns to smooth out the steps, ending with the back of the neck.

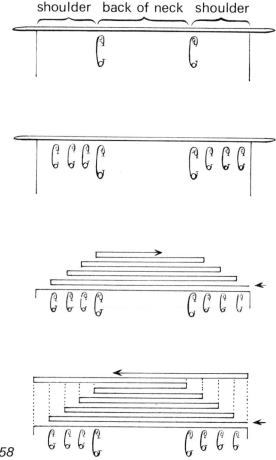

Figure 58

Making darts

Horizontal darts may be used at the underarms of women's jumpers.

Figure 59   Mark and start these darts as if shaping shoulders, but with proportions appropriate to the position and the wearer. Work 2, 3 or 4 complete rows not only to smooth out the steps already made, but also to reduce the potential strain of the next set.

Work the second part of the dart as a mirror image of the first.

In hand-made garments, all shapings should conform to the individual wearer. More groups of stitches should be marked off if, for example, deeper darts are required. Those wearers with slight figures or square shoulders will find they need fewer groups of stitches.

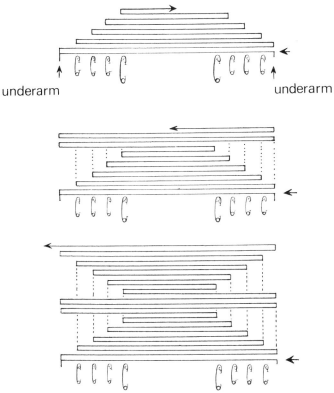

Figure 59

Making vertical openings

Vertical openings are simply gaps between pairs of side edges, and as these consist of the end columns of blocks of rows, vertical openings necessarily involve working to and fro. The edge itself, being part of the frame around the opening, is usually an unshaped knit column.

Armholes in jumpers (*figure 60a*)   Making an opening in a tube means starting to work some of the stitches from the wrong side. This tests the knitter's understanding of the fabric as well as her skill in working it, so make the back of the garment before starting the front which is more conspicuous.

Neck openings (*b*)   Whereas armholes are made in jumpers by working rows instead of rounds; neck openings between armholes are made by working short rows instead of long ones.

If the parts should be symmetrical, make both at the same time on the same needles, using a second ball of yarn. Never leave such rows half way, for the direction of work is not obvious when, at re-starting, working ends are found side by side.

Ribbon slots (*c*)   These are the gaps between narrow blocks of stitches. Make the blocks in turn, carrying the uncut yarn down the length of the slit, then incorporating it into the next edge column.

Vertical buttonholes (*d*)   Work the main set of stitches to the depth of the hole, then work the block of stitches between the hole and the edge of the garment, as though between ribbon slots. Make fewer rows in the edge block than in the main set of stitches, to offset the pull of the button.

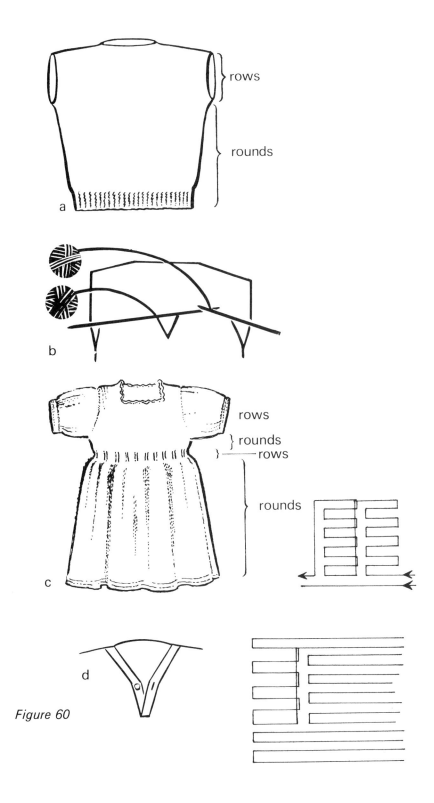

rows

rounds

a

b

rows

} rounds

— rows

rounds

c

d

Figure 60

Making horizontal openings

The 'silk' used for making horizontal openings and for holding their edges together is the knitter's equivalent of tacking cotton. Real knitting silk is even more rarely used than real tacking cotton, but any substitute should have the same strength and slippery surface. In descriptions, the slippery yarn will be called 'silk' and shown wound onto card. The main yarn will be called 'wool' and shown wound into a ball.

Making a thumb in a glove (figure 61)
a Work as far as the division for the thumb, then temporarily ignore the wool.
   b Knit across the gusset stitches in silk and cut off the silk.
   c Transfer the silk stitches. To transfer a stitch (abbr 'tr') move it, unworked and at the normal slope, from rhn to lhn.
   d Continue working the rest of the glove normally in wool until only the thumb remains unknitted.
   e Regain the stitches by weaving a short thin needle into the woollen loops below the silk. Weave another needle into the loops above the silk, including the half-stitch at each end.
   f Firmly pull out the silk. The open slits should be bordered by open loops sloping normally. Restart knitting at one end of the slit, having re-arranged the loops into a tiny triangle. Work both half-stitches, twisting them if they seem large.

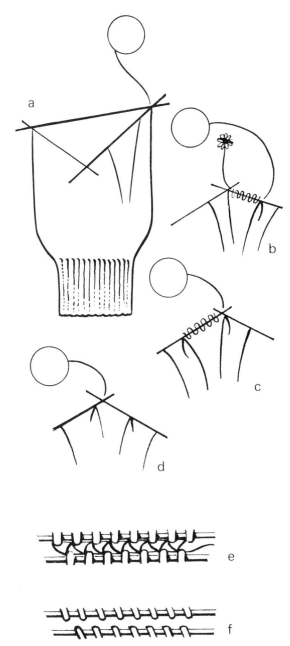

Figure 61

Casting off in silk

This is done so that stitches can be 'held', ie kept safe from the risk of laddering while they are temporarily out of use.

Figure 62a   Let the wool hang out of the way. Use silk to knit two stitches. Take care not to pull the silk right through.

b   Use the tip of lhn to lift the first silk stitch carefully over the second.

c   Set the stitch down clear of both needles. The column below the first stitch is now safe from laddering. *Knit another stitch. Lift the earlier of the two stitches on rhn over the later stitch. Set it down clear of both needles.*

d   Continue until either lhn is empty, or the specified number of stitches has been cast off (remembering that no stitch has been completely cast off until it has been removed from both needles). If any stitches remain on lhn, the loop on rhn counts as the first stitch of the row which is just starting.

e   If lhn is empty, enlarge the loop which remains on rhn until it is a hand-span long. Cut the loop.

f   Leave the tail in the last complete stitch to keep the row safe.

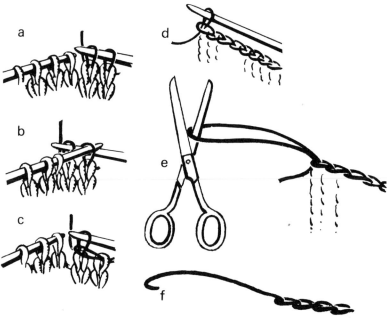

Figure 62

Regaining cast-off loops

This is done when the loops are again required for knitting.

Figure 63   Enlarge the final cast-off loop. Carefully remove from it, then from the final woollen loop, the tail which has been keeping them safe. Insert the tip of a knitting needle into the woollen loop, using, as always when regaining stitches, a thin tool so that the stitch cannot be stretched. Make sure the stitch slopes normally across the needle.

Press the needle tip gently, in the same direction, into the next woollen loop. Gently pull the silk. The two loops are now open and slope normally.

Continue in this way until sufficient loops are again on the needle. If some loops are to remain cast off, draw the silk tail through the next silk loop.

Needle can be held in either
left hand   or   right hand

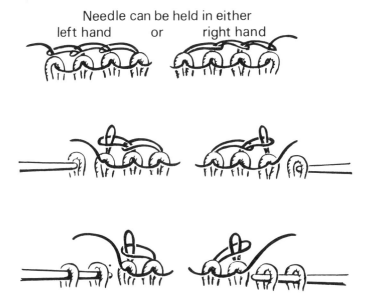

Figure 63

Other ways of holding out-of-use stitches

Small sets of loops can be held on safetypins until they are wanted. With larger groups the end loops might get dragged by safetypins so specially-made stitch-holders may be better, more than one being used if necessary. All the stitches must be transferred back to a working tool before they can be used.

Loops can be held on the working tool itself without having to be transferred but constant vigilance is needed lest the needle fall out, and a long, stiff tool is apt to get in the way of the knitter.

Making a silk cast-on

Figure 64a This is used when columns are to be continuous as from one finger of a glove into the next.

b Work as far as the start of the little finger. Keep the stitches of the little finger on two short needles. Put the stitches of the other fingers on holders. Set aside the glove.

c Prepare a silk cast-on. To do this, use spare needles and silk. Cast on the specified number of stitches. Knit one row, still using silk; cut the silk near to the last stitch and knot the tails together.

d Arrange these silk stitches and the woollen stitches of the little finger to form a tube.

e Use the wool to knit across the silk then on to complete the finger.

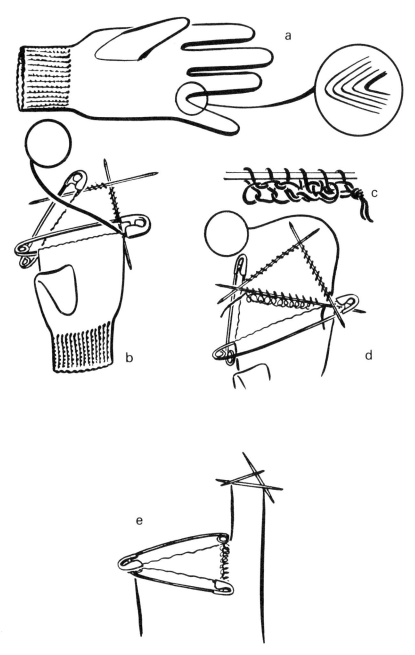

Figure 64

Making use of the silk cast-on

This is used when starting the ring finger of a glove.

Figure 65a Arrange the work so that the silk cast-on is at the top and start to release the bottom row of the little finger from its silk.

b To do this weave a thin knitting needle into every loop of the bottom woollen row.

c Carefully untie the knot beside the last silk stitch. Pull the first silk stitch until most of the cast-on row is released and unpick any remaining stitches.

d The loops of the bottom row are now ready for re-use.

e Prepare to work the ring finger by making another silk cast-on and regaining from their holders the stitches for the front and back of the finger. Re-arrange the four sets of loops among three needles and use a new end of wool to start knitting around the finger.

Work the middle finger similarly.

The first finger is worked entirely on picked-up stitches.

Comparison of top and bottom rows

Removal of a silk cast-on releases the bottom row which, in stocking stitch and a few other fabrics, looks just like the top row and behaves like it. In fabrics such as ribbing, where the yarn has been moved from one surface to the other, the top row is quite different from the bottom row. Loops of the top row can be made to ladder but those of the bottom row can not; though they can be picked up and used for further knitting.

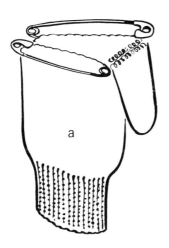

b   c   d

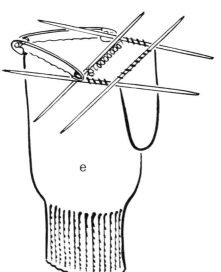

Figure 65

Making a silk-linked cast-on

This is used, for example, in starting a garter stitch collar made in a long narrow strip.

Figure 66a   Cast-on and cast-off rows look different but top and bottom edges can look exactly the same.

b   Use wool and fairly thick needles to cast on the specified number of stitches. Temporarily ignore the wool.

c   If working in rows, push the cast-on stitches to the other end of the needle.

d   Starting from that tip and using silk, knit one round or row. Cut off the silk.

e   Use the working end of wool, now at hand, to knit one round or row. Continue according to instructions.

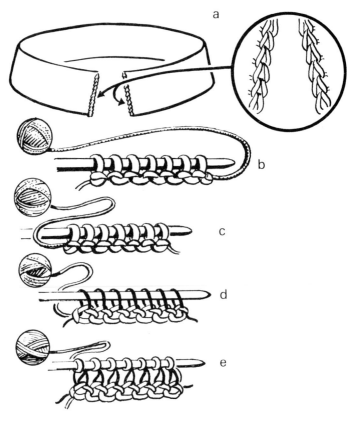

Figure 66

Making use of the silk-linked cast-on

Figure 67a   Reverse the work so that the cast-on row is at the top. Weave a thin needle into every loop of the bottom woollen row.

   b   Pull out the silk. The loops of the bottom row are ready to be cast off. The cast-on row which is, in effect, a crochet chain, is now attached to the bottom row at one end only. Pull undone the cast-on chain.

If the yarn is crinkly hold it carefully in a jet of steam to straighten it.

   c   Use this piece of yarn to cast off the stitches of the bottom row.

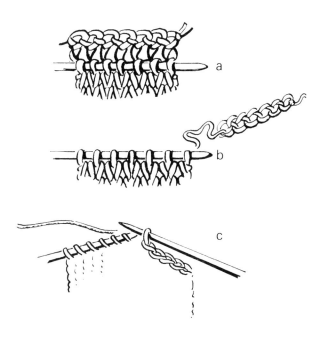

Figure 67

Casting off

This means converting a set of open loops into a chain-like selvedge by lifting the earlier of two worked stitches over the other and then repeating the operation. The chain rests on, and is tilted by the yarn which is carried from stitch to stitch (*figure 68*).

(a) KNITWISE (keeping yarn at back of work, as for silk cast-off) lifting the stitch over

front   back

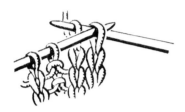 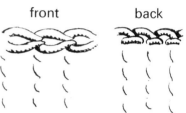

(b) PURLWISE (keeping yarn at front of work) lifting the stitch over

front   back

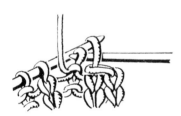 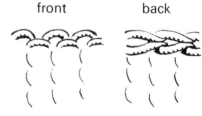

(c) RIBWISE (shifting yarn from surface to surface between stitches)   (d) DETAIL

front   back   top

   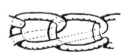

Figure 68

Continuity of cast-off edges

Even when a garment consists of several pieces joined together, the cast-off edges can seem continuous provided the rows are chosen so that all the stitches point in the same direction and the method is chosen so that all parts tilt similarly.

Tightness of cast-off edges

Cast-off edges are caught back on themselves, so their 'give' is limited. Edges which are too tight can make a garment unwearable but these can be avoided if the final yarn is kept intact until the garment has been tested and, if necessary, the cast-off row undone and re-worked more loosely.

A cast-off row can be kept loose by using a larger needle or by occasionally lifting a linking bar, working it and lifting the previous stitch over the new one.

Types of welt

The edge areas of garments are the parts which are most likely to wear out or be pulled out of shape so they are often worked on thin needles to make them dense and strong. Even when fabric is the same throughout, welts almost always look different; they are conspicuously different when the garment consists mainly of a fabric which curls, for welts must stay flat.

The choice of welts affects the character of a garment for if they are non-springy, eg hems or moss stitch (*figure 69*), the garment looks tailored whereas a springy fabric such as ribbing gives the snug fit which is characteristic of knitting, the difference of effect being so great that normally the same type of welting is used at all edges of the garment.

The working of welts is straightforward in long-sleeved high-necked jumpers where the ridges of ribbing are continuous with the columns of the main fabric, or in tailored garments, but more planning is required when welts are needed at row ends, as around sleeveless armholes or lower necklines.

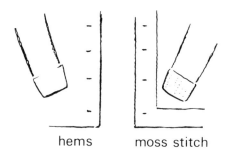

hems   moss stitch

Figure 69

The springy edges which are so easily made by working the ends of the rows in garter stitch (*figure 70*) look nothing like the waist ribbing but (*figure 71*) armhole and neck welts can be springy and also look like the waist ribbing if the rest of the garment is finished first and then the bends at row ends are picked up and are used as the first round of a ribbed tube.

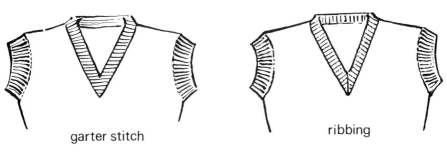

garter stitch   ribbing

Figure 70   *Figure 71*

The welts at the front openings of buttoned jumpers or of cardigans (*figure 72*) need to be firm, not springy, and as ribbing is stiff along its ridges though springy across them, it is almost invariably used for these buttonstands, the ridges being continuous with those of waist and neck.

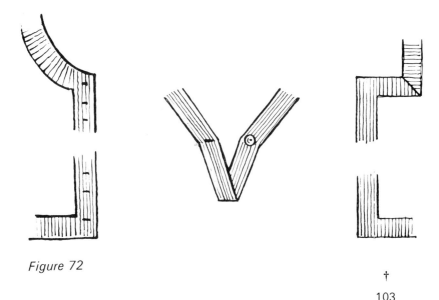

Figure 72

†

Working side welts

This may be done when the buttonstands of a cardigan are made in one with the main fabric. Two thick needles (or pins) and three thin ones (preferably short), are required.

   Figure 73a   *Use a thin needle to work across the welt. Keep the emptied needle handy.

   b   Use a thick needle to continue across the main fabric.

   c   Use the emptied thin needle to continue across the welt at the end of the row.*

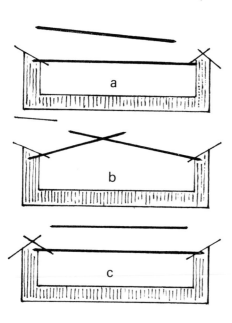

Figure 73

Making buttonholes in welts

These are simply horizontal slits with selvedges above and below.

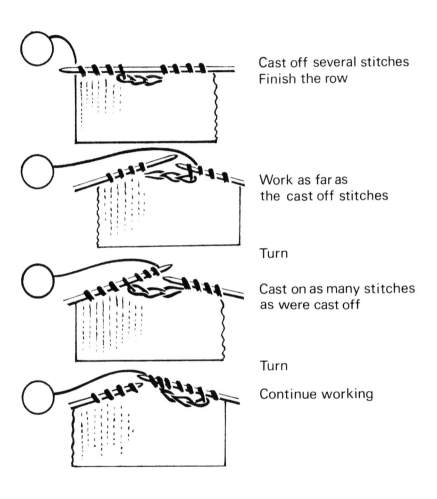

Cast off several stitches
Finish the row

Work as far as
the cast off stitches

Turn

Cast on as many stitches
as were cast off

Turn

Continue working

Figure 74

Slip stitches

Abbreviation 'S' or 'sl'. To slip a stitch, move it, unworked, from lhn to rhn. It is the reverse of a transfer.

Figure 75a When slipped purlwise, the stitch remains at the normal slope. When slipped knitwise (*b*), the stitch slopes abnormally so this is only done when particularly instructed.

Figure 75

Slip stitch edge columns

These edge columns are worked on alternate rows only, to give a chain-like effect. Sometimes pattern leaflets specify whether edges are to be worked in stocking stitch or slip stitch; often knitters make the choice themselves.

Slipping the last stitch of a row is more likely to give a firm edge than slipping the first, for when a stitch is still attached to the working end it can easily be enlarged (*figure 76a*).

When side edges meet they usually look best if they are alike. The appearance of the edge column is affected by the character of the adjacent column; knit stitches tilting it one way and purl the other.

Slip stitch edges and cast off rows look so similar that together they can form a frame which seems continuous (*figure 76b*).

Figure 76a   *b*

Using slip stitches

With the aid of slip stitches, *tubes* can be made using knitting pins. Cast on an even number of stitches. Work *K1. Bring yarn to front (abbr yf). S1. Take yarn to back (abbr yb).*

Figure 77   Slip stitches are often used for making *decorative fabrics*.

   a   A stiff fabric, worked on an even number of stitches.

Row 1   K1, *yf, sl, yb, k1* till 1 rem k1.
Row 2   P1, *yb, sl, yf, p1* till 1 rem p1.

(The stitches before and after the repeat signs make the frame.)

   b   Slip stitch columns. Mark any specified columns. Slip the stitches of the marked columns on alternate rows.

   c   Shadow checks, worked on a multiple of four stitches for the fabric and two for the frame.

Row 1   K1, *s2, k2* k1.
Row 2   P1, *p2, s2* p1.

Work rows 3 and 4 and each alternate pair of rows in knit fabric.

Row 5   K1, *k2, s 2* k1.
Row 6   P1, *s2, p2* p1.

(This placing of centres of repeats above divisions between repeats is called *staggering*.)

   d   Vertical ridges of stocking stitch, worked on a multiple of four stitches for the fabric and one for the frame.

Row 1   K1, *s3, k1*
Row 2   P1, *s3, p1*
Rows 3 and *4*   St st.

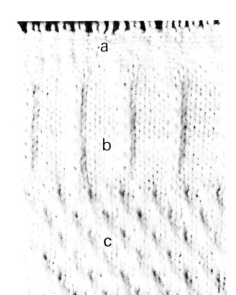

a

b

Figure 77

c

d

Making superimposed side welts

These may be used, for example, at buttoned neck openings.

To start the first part (*figure 78*), *a* mark the centre of the garment, mark the outlines of the welt so that half its stitches are on each side of the centre. Use a thick needle to work across the centre to the marked column. Turn. Use a thin needle to work in rib across the welt columns. Use a thick needle to work the rest of the row.

b Work 6 rows altogether, using thin and thick needles in turn.

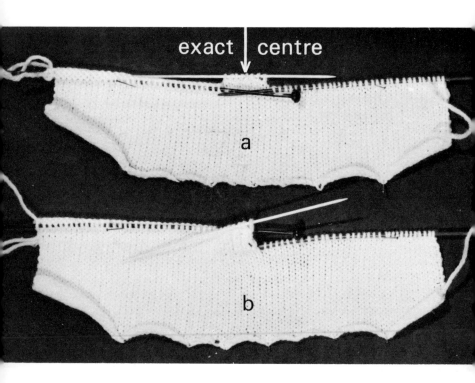

Figure 78

To start the second part (*figure 79a*), use a thin knitting needle to pick up the bars below the first row of welt stitches and below one column beyond. Find a second end of yarn, (it can usually be drawn from the middle of the ball), leave a tail a hand-span long. Work in rib across the new set of welt stitches, using a thin needle and making sure that the edges are symmetrical and that similar columns are superimposed.

b Continue across the second part of the garment, using a thick needle for the main fabric. Work 6 rows altogether on this part, using thin and thick needles in turn. Continue working symmetrically across the two parts, using two thick and three thin needles.

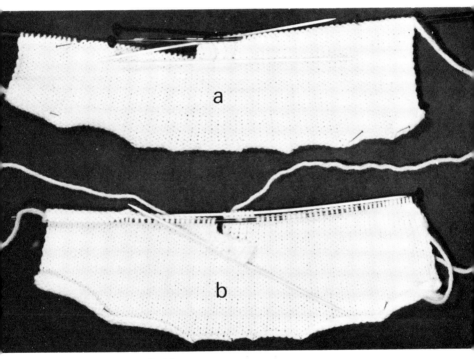

a shows 'wrong' side

Figure 79

†

Removing one stitch

This means drawing one loop through two stitches of the previous row. Both symmetrical versions can be worked easily on the knit surface, but only one is straightforward on the purl surface.

A removal sloping from lower left to upper right
Figure 80a   Insert rhn knitwise into the pair of loops as if they were one.

   b   Draw the yarn forward as a knit stitch. Both original loops have been knitted. These instructions are given as 'knit 2 together' (abbr 'K2 tog').

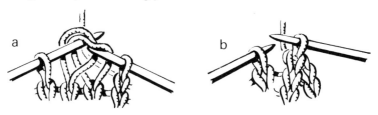

Figure 80

A removal sloping from upper left to lower right
Figure 81a   Insert rhn knitwise into the first loop of the pair. Instead of knitting it, slip it. It slopes abnormally across rhn. Knit the second loop of the pair.

   b   Lift the bar of the slipped stitch and set it down *behind* the knit stitch.

   c   This completes the knitting of the first loop of the pair. These instructions are given as 'Slip 1, knit 1, pass the slip stitch over the knit stitch' (abbr 'S1 K1 psso').

Figure 81

A removal on the purl surface
Figure 82 Insert rhn purlwise into the two loops as if they were one. Twist yarn and rhn together. Press rhn away until one new purl stitch emerges. Turn the work over to make sure the removal is in the correct column and that the slope is from *lower left to upper right.*

Figure 82

Removing a stitch may affect:
1 the number of stitches in the row
2 the appearance of the knit surface of the fabric
3 the shape of the fabric
4 the shape of the row
5 the continuity of the fabric if rows of open loops are joined

Removals used symmetrically to shape fabric

Symmetry will only be perfect if the slipped stitch is set down *behind* the knit stitch, not beside it.

Figure 83 shows removals used to close tubes as in paired toes of socks.

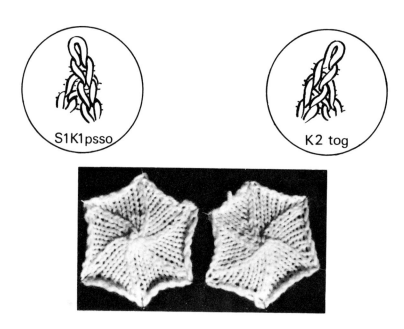

Figure 83

Figure 84 shows removals used near edges, to shape a neckline (*top*); and used within the fabric to make darts ▶ (*centre*); and to make gussets (*bottom*).

S1 K1 psso
K2 tog

1 K1 psso
K2 tog

K2 tog
S1 K1 psso

2 tog
S1 K1 psso

S1 K1 psso
K2 tog

Removals used to shape rows

Making a square neck of a raglan jumper   *Figures 85 a* and *b*
show one of the darts found between the sleeves and body of
a raglan garment. Each dart is made by removing two stitches
symmetrically on each alternate row from armhole to neck welt.

Figure 85a

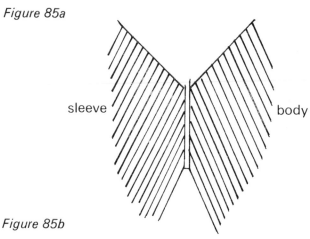

sleeve   body

Figure 85b

Making chevron fabric *Figure 86* (below) Make pairs of removals and pairs of additions alternately so that the columns are short and sloping. The greater the horizontal and the less the vertical separation between shapings, the more sloping the columns and the deeper the undulations at top and bottom edges.

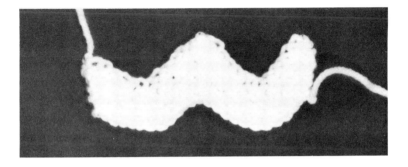

Figure 86

Removals used to make joins

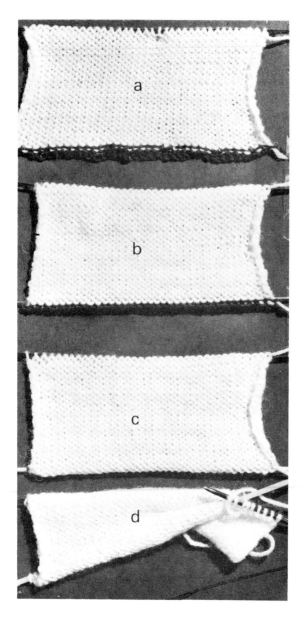

Figure 87

1   Joining rows of loops to make hems which, in knitting, are used to prevent curling not, as in dressmaking, to prevent fraying.

Figure 87a   Start the hem by making a silk cast-on; work the depth of the inner layer of the hem on thin (welt) needles; continue on thick (fabric) needles for the depth of the outer layer of the hem; end with a knit row.

b   Weave a thin needle through the woollen loops of the bottom row.

c   Remove the silk, leaving a row of open loops on the needle.

d   Bring the two needles into contact by folding the hem, right side out. *Purl together the first stitch of the back needle and the first stitch of the front needle. Set down the two purled stitches.*

2   Joining rows of loops to close tubes, eg mitt tips. Arrange the stitches of the back of the hand on one needle and those of the front on another needle. Join front to back by working pairs of stitches together, purlwise, knitwise or ribwise, as though making a hem. Close the columns by casting off each stitch as soon as the next is made.

3   Joining rows to columns to turn french heels.

Figure 88   Make the heel flap by working in knit fabric on half the stitches of the round for as many rows as there are stitches. As with the dutch heel, mark off the stitches into three groups, the outer two exactly equal, the middle group, which becomes the sole flap, the same or slightly wider. Purl across the centre to the marked column. P2 tog. *Turn. S1, k to marked column, sl, k1 psso. Turn. P to marked column, p2 tog.*

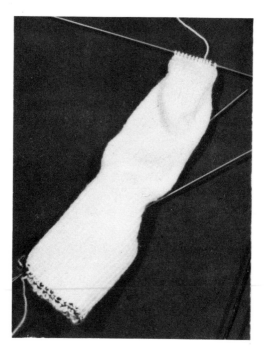

Figure 88

Removals used to shape openings

This method may be used for the thumb of a well-shaped glove (*figure 87*). Use silk to work K2 tog across most of the gusset. Work the palm without further shaping. Later, prepare to work the thumb by regaining all the woollen loops. There will be approximately twice as many below the silk as above it.

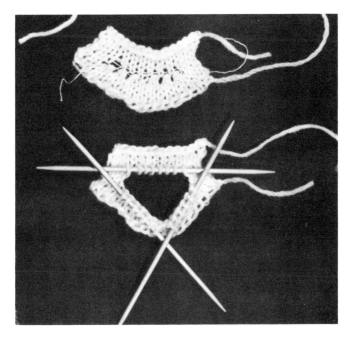

Figure 89

Removing two stitches at one time

This is done when making the point of a V-neck.

Figure 90 The appearance is determined by the choice of top stitch, as seen from the right side.

Decide which of the three stitches is to show on the right side. Put rhn knitwise into that stitch, then, knitwise, into the other stitches in whatever order is most convenient. Finally, draw one new loop through the whole pile.

Follow the same procedure when removing three or more loops.

Left hand stitch on t‹

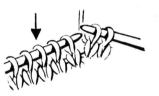

Figure 90

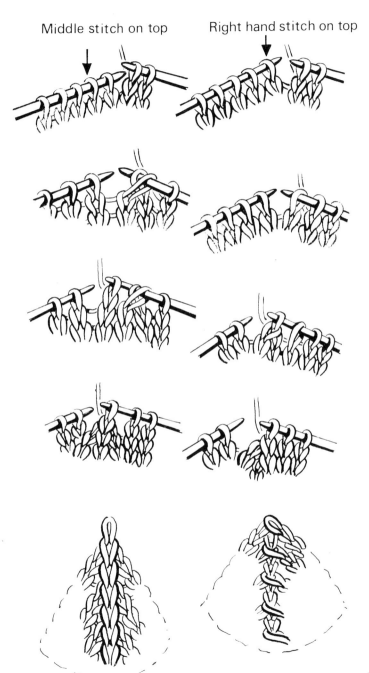

Middle stitch on top   Right hand stitch on top

Making and using Overs

Abbreviation 'O', almost invariably printed as a capital letter. An Over is a turn of yarn made around rhn between columns.

Figure 91 Make an Over after finishing one stitch, by twisting the yarn around rhn in the normal direction before the next stitch is started.

Figure 91

Figure 92 The Over must be worked on the next row or it will become merely a linking bar.

a If worked into the far arm it becomes a lifted linking bar.

b If purled or knitted normally it becomes a small hole surmounted by a new, extra, column.

c If made next to a removal it becomes a small buttonhole, re-inforced on one side but with no additional column to interrupt the rhythm of the fabric.

d If used for adding stitches in chevron fabric it is the basis of fan-and-feather lace.

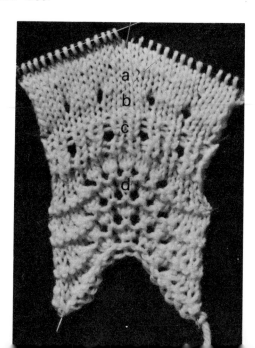

Figure 92

Using an incidental Over as the beginning of the spine of a raglan dart Assemble the sleeves and body on circular or stiff needles. Work one complete round or row to link the parts. On the second round or row (which should be worked from the right side) work across each part in turn until two stitches only of that part remain. K2 tog. Lift on to lhn the linking strand which will have elongated sufficiently to form an Over. Knit or purl into the Over. S1 K1 psso, (*figure 93*).

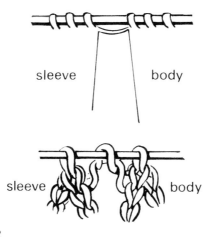

Figure 93

Making and using Enlarged stitches

Abbreviation   'E'. An Enlarged stitch is an extra turn of yarn made around rhn when it is within a stitch.

   Figure 94a   To make an Enlarged stitch, work normally but make two (or more) turns of yarn round rhn.

Figure 94a

If treated as a normal stitch it eventually becomes merely a normal stitch, (see *figure 94b* below). If slipped purlwise for one or more rows and then worked it becomes an elongated stitch. If slipped knitwise for several rows and then worked it becomes a twisted elongated stitch. If slipped for several rows, knitwise or purlwise, and then worked before or after its original column, it becomes a slanted elongated stitch. When two or more stitches are worked into it, it becomes a wide stitch with two or more columns above it. The extra turn of yarn which enlarges the stitch becomes, in effect, three extra bars and can give rise to at least three extra columns without strain.

Neither two knit stitches nor two purl stitches can be worked consecutively and directly into any loop. It is possible and usual to use knit and purl stitches alternately.

Figure 94b

†

Grafting

This means sewing pieces together in imitation of knitted fabric. Practice with stocking stitch first then, when other fabrics have to be joined, use the same practice methods to study them.

Use a wool or tapestry needle for the sewing because its eye is large enough to take wool and its tip blunt enough to slip easily into stitches without splitting yarn.

Preparation for practice Use wool to make a strip 9 columns wide and 6 rows deep. Push the work to the other tip of the needle. Work one row in silk and 6 more in wool. Repeat these 7 rows before each stage of practice.

Practice   Figure 95 (opposite)   *a* Study the track of the silk through the woollen loops.

b   Use a threaded needle to follow exactly in the track of the silk.

c   Cut one arm of a silk stitch near the centre of the row. Unpick two or three stitches each side of the cut to make a short slit. Close the slit by stitching with wool as though in the track of the silk.

d   Carefully unpick a whole row of silk then replace it with wool. Apart from tails the fabric should seem continuous. The loops have been grafted together.

e   Weave short thin needles into the woollen rows above and below the silk. Remove the silk row. Graft the loops directly from the needles.

f   Finally, make two short strips of the fabric and graft them together. this time top row to top row using the working end of one of the strips.

The secret of successful grafting is a careful study of the original fabric. *Stocking stitch* can be grafted top or bottom, to top or bottom, so that the join does not show. *Garter stitch*, also, can be grafted top or bottom to top or bottom so that the join does not show, but the rows have to be suitably chosen.

All fabrics can be joined top row to bottom row as though the work had been continuous. Any two fabrics can be grafted in any direction and the join can seem to be a continuation of one of the fabrics. All fabrics can be grafted top row to top row to make a join which feels as springy as the rest of the fabric but which may not be invisible.

126

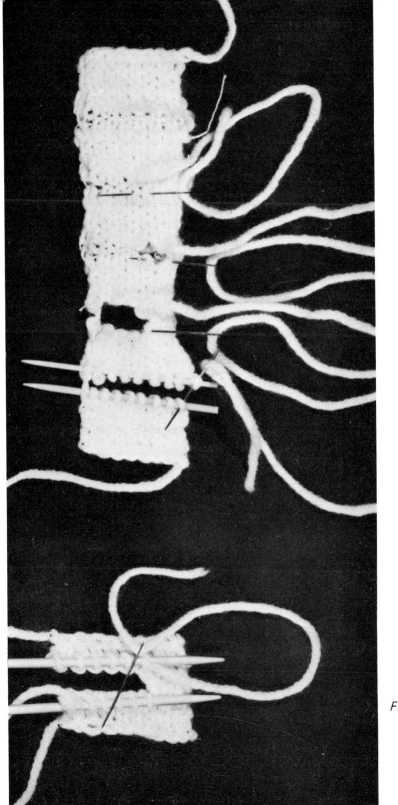

a

b

c

b

e

f

Figure 95

Linked loop join

This is a method of joining rows of open loops by using a crochet hook to draw loops of each row alternately through those of the other (*figure 96*). The join looks different from the fabric but is quickly made and is springy. It is useful for joining surfaces which will be flattened together, such as lapels or hanging pockets.

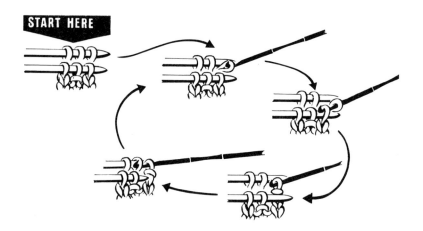

Figure 96

Making hanging pockets

A hanging pocket is much like a knitted thumb but larger and turned inside out.

Prepare the slit by working a row of silk the width of the proposed pocket. Later, regain the stitches above and below the slit, re-arrange them in a triangle and knit a short tube. Carefully turn the tube to the wrong side of the garment. (The knit surface is now inside the tube.) Rearrange the stitches on two needles so that the pocket lies flat against the main fabric.

Close the tube with a linked loop join.

Using stocking stitch edges

Stocking stitch edges can be used at the beginning of the springy welts at ribbed armholes. (*Figure 97*) prepare a practice piece using thick tools (to show up details); cast on not more than a dozen stitches (only edge columns matter and they must be knit columns), and use rib (to obviate curl). Work a dozen rows, noticing how yarn gets from the end of one row to the start of the next. Study the edge columns. Identify the pips along the edges. Hold a safety-pin or, preferably, a knitting pin knob upward, against each edge column. Continue the strip but take the yarn around the pin at the end of each row. Work several rows in this way.

Identify the bends of yarn rising from the end of each row to the start of the next. Relate these bends to the pips and study the edge columns. They are not distorted. Work several rows without the pins. Notice how the bends are pulled awry to form pips, and how this distorts the column.

Pick up a bend by pointing a thin needle up the purl surface of an edge column, lifting the pip and scooping up the strand beneath. Experiment until the result is identical with the bends made around the pin.

Sloping edges, eg V-necks, usually need more stitches than there are bends so occasionally two stitches have to be worked into one bend. It is best to follow a normal knit stitch by a purl made into the back arm of the bend.

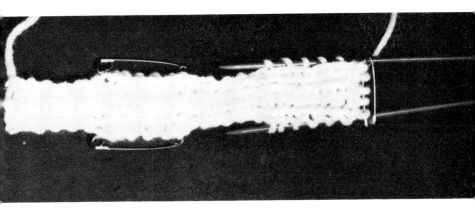

Figure 97

Lifted ladder linkage

This is a method of joining side edges of those fabrics which cannot be worked in rounds, eg vertical stripes of colour or Argyle diamonds; or of parts of garments which cannot be made all in one because of the limitations of machine knitting or of difficulties of knitting in trains! The join feels as springy as knit fabric and looks just like it, whereas sewn joins do not.

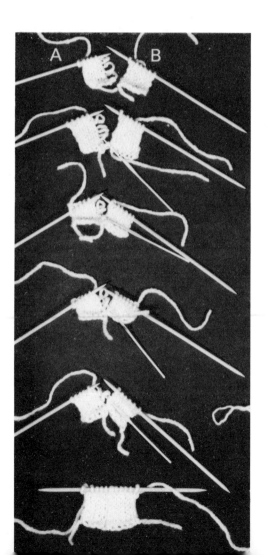

Figure 98

Figure 98 Release the final stitch of the row from the needle and let the edge column of piece A ladder completely. This will only happen if all the stitches are unshaped and unsplit. (If the rungs seem to be losing their identity keep them on a holder or thick pin.)

Insert a crochet hook into the edge stitch of the bottom row of B. Hook the bottom rung of A. Draw the rung through B as a loop on the crochet hook. *Insert the hook into the edge stitch of the next row of B. Hook up the next rung of A. Pull this through the edge of B and through the loop already on the hook.* Continue in this way to the top of the column. Treat the top loop like the rest of its row.

This method may also be used for joining side hems and buttonstands.

Figure 99 Mark the column where the join will be made.

a Let the edge column ladder. Working from the right side, pick up the rungs of the laddered edge through the stitches of the marked column. Turn the work over at each stitch to make sure the correct rung has been picked up.

b Complete the hem in this way.

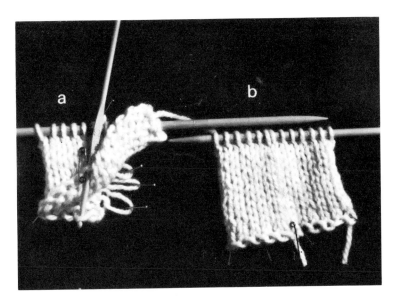

Figure 99

131

Making hemmed welts

The broken lines in these diagrams indicate the omission of many of the central columns.

1 *Straight method Figure 100* *a* Use silk cast-on to start the bottom hem. Use thin needles and wool to work the under layers of the hem. Use silk cast-on to start the two layers of each side hem. Using wool, work both eventual under layers on thin needles and the rest of the stitches on thick needles.

b When the depth of the bottom hem has again been worked knit or purl its edges together and continue upward.

c Later, fold the side hems and join the lower edges by linking loops, join side hems to bottom hem by lifted ladder on wrong side, and side hems to main fabric by lifted ladder on right side.

1 Straight method

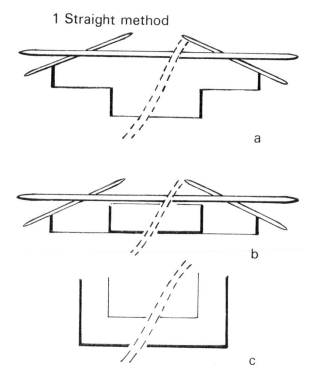

a

b

c

Figure 100

2 *Mitred method* *Figure 101* *a* Prepare a silk cast-on for the whole width of the work. Use wool to work one row across the whole silk row then use thin needles to work the under layer of the bottom hem including progressively more stitches on each row. Use thick needles for the outer layer of the bottom hem, and thin needles for the side hems which are just starting.

b When all cast-on columns are in use, make a knitted join of the bottom hem.

c Later, join the mitre with linked loops and the side hem with a lifted ladder.

2 Mitred method

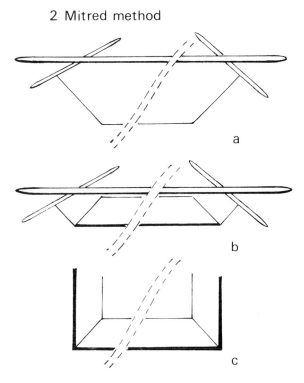

a

b

c

Figure 101

Making buttonholes in side hems

Figure 102 a Prepare horizontal slits, closed with silk, in the equivalent columns of both layers of the hems. Weave thin needles through the four sets of loops. Remove the silk.

b Fold the hem, bringing the sets of open loops into contact. Link those of the outer layer to those of the inner layer by the linked loop method, working across the top of each slit then below it. No tail is available for holding the final loop of this join, so use a separate piece of yarn to sew it between the layers of the hem.

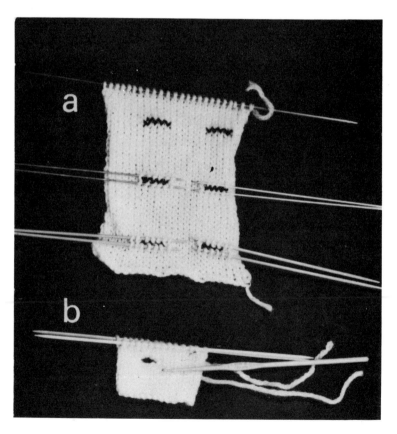

Figure 102

Shaping a side hem

This is done when making the sloping V-neck of a jacket for if the hem is to fit well at the angle there should be more rows in the fold column than in the columns involved in the join.

Figure 103   a Mark the fold column. Make a semi-mitre in both layers of the hem.

b   Move the marker pin to the column through which the hem will be joined. Keeping the hem always the same depth, make it slope by removing stitches from beside the marked column. Fold the hem and join it by the lifted ladder method.

c   Examine the wrong side for correctness of joining.

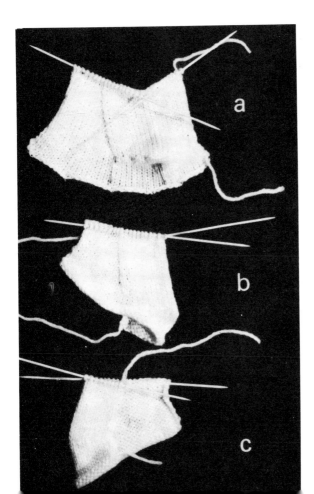

Figure 103

†

Making use of tails

Even when knitting seems finished, the yarn should be kept intact until accuracy and fit have been finally approved; a second version may take more yarn than the first.

Each tail must be darned in eventually, but if it is long enough and in the right place, it may be of use before it is hidden away (*figures 104* and *105*).

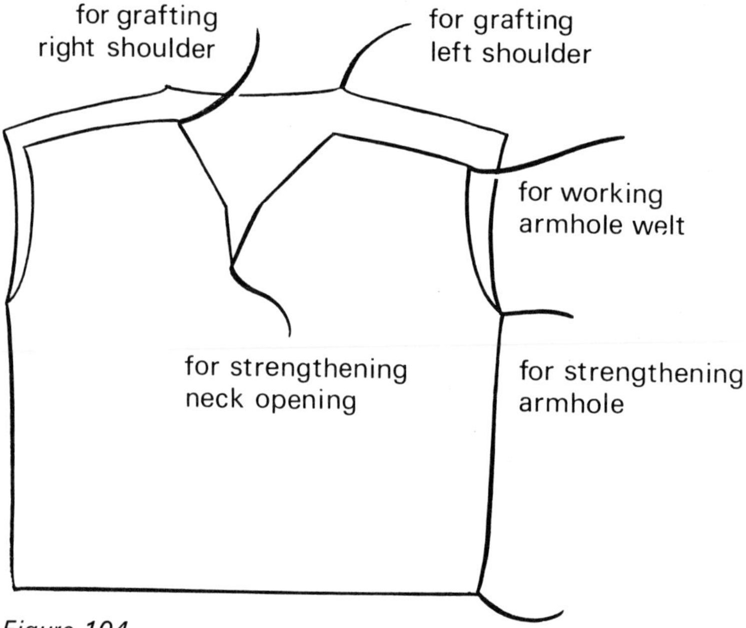

for grafting
right shoulder

for grafting
left shoulder

for working
armhole welt

for strengthening
neck opening

for strengthening
armhole

Figure 104

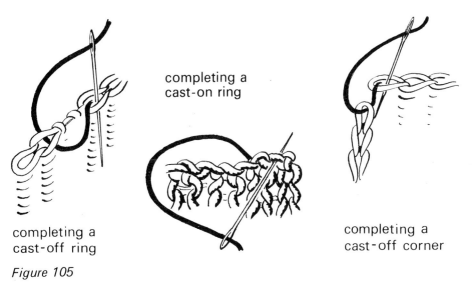

completing a
cast-on ring

completing a
cast-off ring

completing a
cast-off corner

Figure 105

Hiding the tails

Finally, thread the tail on a tapestry needle and stitch under the arms of a column of knit stitches. If possible, stitch in this way to the nearest change of fabric. If the column is short, or the region is likely to be subject to strain, stitch to the edge again, using a different set of arms (*figure 106*).

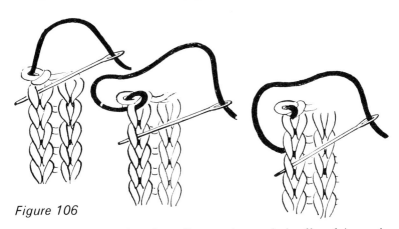

Figure 106

In experienced hands, tails can be ended off safely and invisibly by oversewing, as in needlework, but great care is needed.   †

Pressing

If lubricated with steam, snagged fibres can float back into place letting the stitches resume their correct shape. Pressing is best done when the garment is complete except for buttons.

The process is quite different from the pressing done by dressmakers and tailors; it will not alter the shape permanently though it may do so temporarily.

When pressing smooth surfaces, the aim is to flatten the fabric while steaming it, so use a table large enough to take the full spread of the garment, so that the steam is not dissipated by manipulation.

Figure 107 Spread a single ironing blanket and sheet on the table. Double the garment (so that the steam is trapped between the layers) knit side outermost, and spread it flat on the table. Place a thin, damp (not wet) cloth on the garment. Avoiding folds rest the iron lightly on the cloth. When the cloth is dry, lift the iron and rest it on another part. Dampen the cloth again as necessary.

Re-fold the garment and press the parts which have been near the folds, previously avoided.

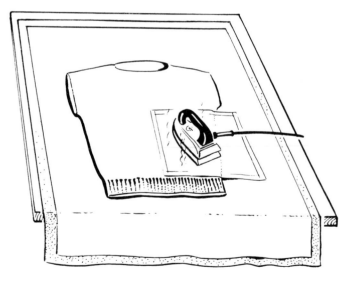

Figure 107

When pressing raised patterns, the aim is not merely to avoid flattening embossed work, but if possible, to increase the three-dimensional effect by inflating the raised portions with steam.

Figure 108 Arrange a single layer, embossed surface downward, on several layers of very soft blanket, cover it with a thin, damp cloth and apply the iron lightly so that it cannot flatten.

Figure 108

Figure 109 Lengthen springy welts while the steam is still in them.

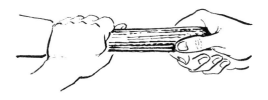

Figure 109

Washing knitted garments

These instructions are suggested for woollen garments which might be damaged by machine washing.

Figure 110   Place the garment in a net or bag made of thin material. Immerse this in a large bowl of warm lather. Swirl the bag around in the water. Lift it and remove the dirty water by squeezing the bag gently. Do not wring. Repeat the operations using successive bowls of fresh suds until the water remains fairly clean.

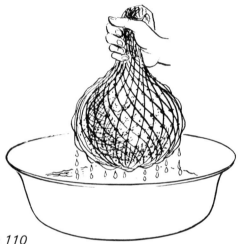

Figure 110

Rinse it in several changes of clear warm water, squeezing it well between rinses. Repeat this until the water remains fairly clear.

Figure 111   Remove excess water by rolling the bag in a towel or by spinning it for a very short time in a dryer.

Remove the bag but never leave the garment unsupported.

Figure 111

Support the garment either from within on an inflatable dummy or on a Shetland woollie horse or from below on a hammock. *Figure 112.*

Dry the garment outside in a breeze if possible and out of direct sunshine which might cause fading. Never dry wool by direct heat from a fire.

If ribbed welts have widened, at this or any other time, moisten them and pull them lengthways.

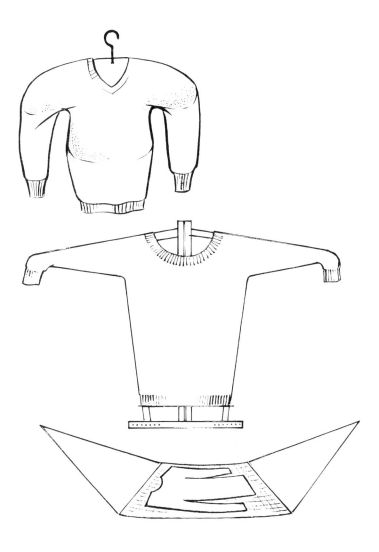

Figure 112

†

A knitter's equipment

This should eventually include as complete a selection as possible of straight and circular knitting needles. Also
A selection of knitting pins
Tool gauges
Stitch-holders of various types and lengths
Crochet hooks
Tapestry needles of various sizes
Safety pins of assorted sizes
Rulers and tape measures
A pair of small, sharp-pointed scissors
'Silk'
A collection of oddments of yarn for practice and experiments.

Conclusion

Anyone who has knitted the three kinds of garment described and worked the preliminary trial pieces needed for each of them in turn can feel she has been well and truly introduced to the craft and is quite ready to deepen her acquaintance with it. There is much else for her to try, and all of it exciting . . . new yarns, new fabrics, new shapes, new ways of shaping, new manipulations to be invented, new and better patterns to be found, new and better ways of interpreting them and, best of all, creation of new garments with every stitch planned by the knitter to suit her own needs, and all perfectly knitted.

Sleeveless pullover

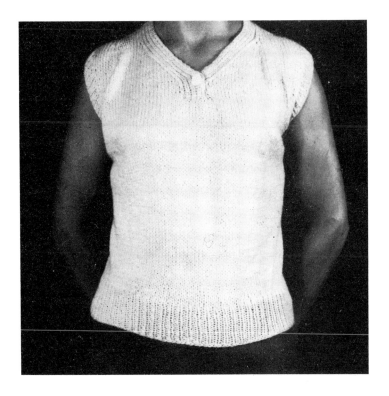

Pattern for sleeveless pullover

Requirements   DK wool, at least 400 yards (6 to 8 oz) (370 metres). 1 circular needle, size 6, length 24 in. (60 cm) to be used for all st st. 1 circular needle, size 8, length 24 in. (60 cm) and 1 set needles, size 8, length 8 in. (200 mm) used for all ribbing. 1 button.

Measurements   Bust 32 in. (80 cm).
Stitch size   5 cols and 6½ rows per inch (25 mm), on size 6 needles.

Cast on 148st. Join into a tube. Work 18 rounds *K1 p1*.
Change to st st, k 3 rounds.
Round 4   K24, add 1, k1, add 1, k21, add 1, k1, add 1, k to end of round, (152)
Rounds 5 and 6   Knit.
Round 7   K25, add 1, k1, add 1, k23, add 1, k1, add 1, k to end of round, (156)
Rounds 8 and 9   Knit.
Round 10   K26, add 1, k1, add 1, k25, add 1, k1, add 1, k to end of round, (160)
Rounds 11 – 43   Knit.
Round 44   K83, turn, p83, turn, k79, turn, p75, turn, k70, turn, p65, turn, k60, turn, p55, turn, k to end of round.
Rounds 45 and 46   Knit.
Round 47   K69, turn, p55, turn, k60, turn, p65, turn, k70, turn, p75, turn, k79, turn, p83, turn, k to end of round.
Round 48   Knit.
Round 49   K151. Hold 101 st for underarms and fronts.

BACK   Continue in st st on remaining 59 st for 44 rows.

SHOULDERS   P56, turn, k53, turn, p49, turn, k45, turn, p41, turn, k37, turn, p to end of row. K 1 row. P47.
Hold 12 st from each end of row for shoulders.
Work 6 rows ribbing on remaining 35 st. Cast off.

RIGHT FRONT   Keep on holders the 17 st of each underarm and the 30 st of the left front. Regain 37 st for right front.
Row 1   Starting at armhole, p36, s1.
Row 2   *K1 p1* 3 times. K to end.
Rows 3 – 7   Continue in st st with ribbed welt and slip st edge.
Row 8   K1, p1, s1, k1, psso, O, k1, p1, turn, k1, p1, k1, p1, k1, s1, turn, *k1 p1* twice, turn, k1, p1, k1, s1, turn, *k1 p1* 3 times, k to end of row.
Row 9   P31, *k1 p1* twice, k1, s1.

Row 10   *K1 p1* 3 times, s1, k1, psso, k29.

Continue similarly, removing 1 st below welt on alternate rows.

Row 20   (6th removal row) *K1 p1* 3 times, s1, k1, psso, k13, k2tog, s1, k1, psso, k7.

Continue, removing 1 st below welt on alternate rows and also removing 2 st from shoulder dart on every 6th row.

Rows 33 – 47   Continue in unshaped st st with ribbed welt and slip st edge.

Row 48   *K1 p1* 3 times, k10, turn, p10, k1, p1, k1, p1, k1, s1, turn, *k1 p1* 3 times, k6, turn, p6, k1, p1, k1, p1, k1, s1.

Row 49   *K1 p1* 3 times, k13.

Row 50   P13, k1, p1, k1, p1, k1, s1.

Cut yarn leaving a long enough tail to graft the shoulder stitches. Hold the stitches.

LEFT FRONT   Hold the 17 st for each underarm. Regain remaining 30 st for left front. Pick up 7 st from under welt.

Row 1   Starting at welt, *p1 k1* 3 times, p31.

Rows 2 – 6   Continue in st st with ribbed welt and slip st edge. Continue as for right front, omitting buttonhole, and reversing shapings. End with the purl row.

Use the tails to graft shoulder fronts to shoulder backs.

ARMHOLES   Regain 17 st from underarm. Pick up all bends around armholes. Work *k1 p1* working 2 st into every third bend. Continue ribbing, keeping both corners of underarm in purl and on alternate rows working 2 st together before and after these purl columns. Complete 6 rounds ribbing altogether. Cast off.

Darn in ends. Press. Sew on button.

NOTE

On pages 62, 73, 83, 87, 99, 103, 109, 125, 128, 135, 137 and 141 the sign † indicates that a set of descriptions has been completed and the newly acquired skills should next be worked into the garment. Once knitting has started, an unfamiliar instruction should take the knitter from the garment back to the text until the next set of skills has been mastered. See also pages 146 and 147.

Box diagram of sleeveless pullover

Requirements   DK wool, at least 400 yards (6 to 8 oz), 1 circular needle, size 6, length 24 in. (60 cm) to be used for all st st. 1 circular needle, size 8, length 24 in. (60 cm) and 1 set of needles size 8, length 8 in. (200 mm) used for all ribbing. 1 button.
Measurements   Bust 32 in. (80 cm).
Stitch size   5 cols and $6\frac{1}{2}$ rows per inch (25 mm), on size 6 needles.
See note on page 145

		Cast off
52	35	
		* K1 P1* for back of neck
46	59	
		Work and smooth shoulder slopes
44	59	
		Mark cols 4, 8 and 12 from each end
44	59	
		St st
0	59	
Back		Hold last 9 st of round then 8 of next for
		armhole +67 for front and 17 for second armhole
68	160	
		St st
66	160	
		Work and smooth underarm darts
62	160	
		Mark cols 5, 10 and 15 in front of each underarm
62	160	
		St st
29	160	
		On this and each 3rd row add 1 st each side
		of each dart
22	148	
		Mark cols 1 and 71 as underarms. Mark
		cols 25 and 47 for bust darts
22	148	
		St st
19	148	
		* K1 P1* as tube
1	148	
		Cast on
0	0	
Start		

Darn in tails   Press   Sew on button

Cast off

		Instructions
6	70	*K1 P1* removing 1 st each side of each corner purl on alt rows
1	82	Pick up bends and regain underarm st. Keeping underarm corner st in purl, work *K1 P1*, adding to bends as necessary
0	0	

Armholes

Graft shoulders and their welts

49	38	Work and smooth shoulder slopes
47	38	

Mark cols 4 and 8 from armhole edges

47	38	Maintain st st and welt
33	38	Remove 1 from each side of each dart on this and each 6th row 3 times while continuing to remove 1 from under each welt on alt rows
19	64	

Mark cols 9 and 10 from each armhole for darts

19	64	Remove 1 st from under each welt on alt rows
9	74	Starting at welt, work 6 rows, then semi-mitre, then finish row
0	74	

Left front

Pick up underwelt and regain st of left front

9	37	Work to neck opening
8	37	Work buttonhole in welt, then semi-mitre
		Finish row at neck opening
7	37	Work in st st with welt of 6 st + slip st edge
1	37	Purl, starting at underarm
0	37	

Right front

Regain st for right half of front

Outline pattern for a pair of ankle socks

Requirements   Use sock yarn, preferably a wool-nylon mixture. 1 oz (about 120 yd, 110 m) should suffice for one sock.
   Use one set of short needles, No. 14 (34).

Preparation   Work a short experimental tube on 90 stitches. Slip it over the foot. Decide how many of its columns are needed to fit that foot, aiming at a multiple of 8 stitches. Use that number to start the welt.

Darn in all tails (137)   Press (138)

Cast off starting edge (100)

Thread tail through remaining 8 loops

On alt rounds rem 8 sts equidistantly

(Make the pair symmetrical)

If necessary, remove stitches at sides of

sole to leave an exact multiple of 8

Knit a tube of sufficient length

*Knit 4 rounds   Rem 1 st each side, keeping

width of instep unchanged* (110)

Rep 2 or 3 times

Re-form tube, picking up all bends at sides

of heel flap (129)

Make sole flap, linking it to final row of

heel flap (118)

Continue in st st

Work square heel flap

Hold half the sts for instep (92)

K1 P1 (50, 51)

Cast on (44, 45), silk-linked (98), for a tube

Start

Numbers in brackets indicate the relevant explanatory pages.

Outline pattern for a pair of gloves

Numbers in brackets indicate the relevant explanatory pages
Requirements
Try dishcloth cotton, sold in $\frac{3}{4}$ lb hanks. Each glove uses about 90 yards (85 m) (14).

Use sets of short needles, Nos 11 and 13 (34).
Instructions
Find the stitch size using No. 11 needles (70, 71). Measure around the hand just above the wrist. Calculate how many stitches are needed.

Cast on (44, 45), silk-linked (98), this number of stitches arranged in a tube (30, 47). Use No. 13 needles to work rib (50, 51) for sufficient depth. Change to No. 11 needles and st st. Work 3 rounds (75).

Decide the position of the thumb (82, 83) and mark gusset outline. On every 4th round add 2 st (80, 81) for gusset until this is wide enough. Continue without shaping until it is long enough. Hold stitches of gusset as a shaped slit (119), if possible leaving a multiple of 9 stitches for the hand. Knit to the level of separation of little finger.

Mark off stitches into 9 fairly equal groups; 3 groups will be used for the index finger, 2 for each of the other fingers. Hold (94) all groups except those of little finger. Cast on, silk-linked, 4 stitches to complete the finger (95). Knit a sufficient length. Complete finger by working reductions at centre of each needle on alternate rounds, each reduction removing two stitches, the centre stitch being on top (121). When 3 remain, K3 tog. Enlarge stitch and cut yarn.

Pick up 4 st from little finger (96, 97); 1 group from each of front and back; cast on, silk-linked, 3 st to complete ring finger. Knit and close finger as before. Repeat for middle finger. No cast on is required for the index finger.

Pick up stitches around thumb (119). Work as for fingers.

Cast off the cast-on round (99, 100). Darn in all tails (137). Press (138).

Glossary

Arm of a stitch   The part of the stitch which is joined to its fellow by the bar at the top of the stitch and to the arm of the next stitch by the linking bar.

Asterisks   These are commonly used in knitting leaflets as repeat signs. All instructions given between two similar signs must be repeated.

Back of stitch   The arm, normally the left, which the knitter cannot see because it is behind the needle.

Back of the work   or of any part of it. The surface which faces away from the knitter.

Bar of the stitch   The part which joins the two arms. The loop hangs by the bar from the needle.

Bend   The strand of yarn rising from the end of one row of plain fabric to the start of the next when the edge column is not distorted.

Botany Wool   An alternative name for Merino wool.

Bottom row   The row worked first, usually into cast-on stitches.

Buttonstands   Strips of firm fabric worked at the sides of openings and usually carrying buttons or their holes.

Cast off   The selvedge at the top of the work.

Cast on   The selvedge at the bottom of the work from which the whole fabric starts.

Circular needle   A knitting tool consisting of two short knitting needles connected by a flexible shaft. It is often slightly longer than its stated length.

Column   A vertical set of stitches which would form a ladder if dropped.

Crimp   The tiny waves which occur naturally along the fibres of most wools, giving bulk to the spun yarn.

Crossbred Wool   A tough, hard-wearing wool.

Dart   A shaping made as though a triangle had been cut from the fabric and the cut edges re-joined.

Decrease   To remove one or more stitches.

Dye lot   All the yarn dyed in one batch. The symbol given to it.

Enlarged stitch   An extra turn of yarn made while a stitch is being worked.

Fabric   Knitted work of a characteristic type and texture.

First Row   The bottom row.

Frame   The single set of unshaped stitches arranged all around a sampler or garment. It usually consists of an edge column each side and the cast-on and cast-off rows below and above. It is useful when side edges have to be joined, particularly when they are so awkwardly shaped that they must be oversewn through the pips or bends.

Front of the work   The surface facing the knitter.

Garter stitch   Springy fabric made by working all rows in knit.

Gathers   The puckering produced when a wider piece of fabric is continued directly into a narrower piece.

Gauge   A piece of equipment for measuring tool thickness.

Grafting   Joining two pieces of knitting by sewing one row in exact imitation of the track of the knitted yarn.

Gusset   A shaping made as though a triangle of fabric had been inserted into a slit in the garment.

Handle (of yarn)   The tactile qualities.

Hem   A welt made by working extra length or width then turning the excess, usually to the wrong side, and fixing it there.

Hold stitches   Keep them safe when they are to be unworked for some time.

Horizontal   Parallel to rows.

Increase   To add one or more stitches.

Knit   To engage in any aspect of knitting. To make a knit stitch.

Knit fabric   The fabric made by working all rounds in knit stitches. Stocking stitch.

Knit stitch   A stitch showing arms only at the front.

Knitwise   Inserted from front to back of a loop on the needle.

Length of Fabric   Measurement along columns.

Line   A set of stitches made by working into some or all of the stitches on a knitting needle before turning to work back.

Linking bar   The link between one stitch and the next.

Loop   Often used as the exact equivalent of *stitch* but more correctly the inverted U-shape of yarn drawn through a stitch of the previous row and still held on the needle.

Merino wool   Soft, fine yarn made from the fleece of merino sheep.

Mitre   A right-angled turn or join.

Moss stitch   A non-curling fabric showing a lattice of bars.

Needle (knitting)   A shaft with two tapered tips. It may be slightly shorter than its stated length.

Needle (tapestry, or wool)   A sewing needle with an eye large enough to hold wool and a tip blunt enough not to split yarn.

Needlebreak   The change from using one needle to the next when working in rounds. The fabric in that region.

Obedient fabric   One which has little inherent shape.

Obedient yarn   One which has little inherent springiness.

Open edge   An edge made of loops which are open and liable to run.

Over   An extra turn of yarn around the needle between columns.

Pattern   An ambiguous word which may mean a printed set of instructions for making a garment, or the instructions themselves, a fabric or the instructions for making it.

Penelope club   A group of knitters (Odyssey. Book XIX.)

Pin (knitting)   A knobbed shaft with a tapered tip.

Pip   A projection from a stocking stitch edge, made when yarn is carried up directly from one row to the next, distorting the edge column.

Plain   Obsolescent term for a knit stitch or knit fabric.

Ply   One of two or more spun strands which are twisted together to form permanently-spun yarn.

Press   To apply warm steam so that snagged fibres can resume their places and stitches can revert to correct shapes.

Purl fabric   The fabric inside a tube made all in knit. Reversed stocking stitch.

Purl stitch   A stitch showing bars only at the front.

Purlwise   Inserted from back to front of a loop on the needle.

Quality   A spinner's term for variation of type, or kind of yarn.

Ribbing   A springy fabric of knit and purl columns alternately.

Right side of the work   The surface intended to be seen.

Row   Synonymous with line.

Selvedge   Any closed edge.

Silk   A general term for the strong yarn with a slippery surface which has many accessory uses in knitting.

Slip   To move a stitch, unworked, from lhn to rhn.

Slip knot   The first loop of many methods of casting on.

Slope of the yarn   across the front of the needle. In the Western European tradition stitches slope from upper left to lower right.

Staggered pattern   One with each motif of a set placed directly over the gap separating those in the previous set.

Stitch   Either a single loop, usually after it has been worked, or a fabric.

Stitch size   The number of columns and of rows in an inch.

Stocking stitch   A fabric which shows only knit stitches.

Strand   A piece of yarn or one of its plies.

Tail of yarn   The short piece of yarn at the start and finish of any piece of knitting.

Tension   The pull exerted on the yarn by the fingers of the knitter. Sometimes a synonym for *stitch size*.

Thickness   The inverse of the length of a strand of known weight.

Top of the work   The part most recently made.

Transfer   To move a loop, unworked, from rhn to lhn.

Tubular knitting   Work done on circular needles or a set of stiff needles so that it progresses always in the same direction.

Turn   To change needles ready to work back, even though both needles still hold stitches.

Vat number   Dye lot.

Vertical   Parallel to columns.

Welt   A band of fabric, single or double, which strengthens an edge.

Width of fabric   Measurement along rows.

Work   An indication of a continuation of activity but not of its nature.

Working end of yarn   The next part to be used.

Wrong side   The surface not intended to be seen during wear.

Yarn   Any knittable strand.

Yarperoz   The length in yards of an ounce of wool and hence, a unit of its thickness.

Abbreviations

alt   alternate
beg   begin(ning)
col   column
dec   decrease
DK   Double Knitting (wool)
E   Enlarged stitch
gs   garter stitch
in.   inch
inc   increase
K   Knit
lhn   left hand needle
ms   moss stitch
m   metre
mm   millimetre
O   Over
P   Purl
psso   pass the slip stitch over
rem   remain or remove
rhn   right hand needle
S   slip
st   stitch(es)
st st   stocking stitch
tr   transfer
yb   yarn back
yd   yard
yf   yarn forward

Index